EVALUATION FOR RISK OF VIOLENCE IN JUVENILES

BEST PRACTICES IN FORENSIC MENTAL HEALTH ASSESSMENT

Series Editors

Thomas Grisso, Alan M. Goldstein, and Kirk Heilbrun

Series Advisory Board

Paul Appelbaum, Richard Bonnie, and John Monahan

Titles in the Series

Foundations of Forensic Mental Health Assessment, *Kirk Heilbrun, Thomas Grisso, and Alan M. Goldstein*

Criminal Titles

Evaluation of Competence to Stand Trial, *Patricia A. Zapf and Ronald Roesch*

Evaluation of Criminal Responsibility, *Ira K. Packer*

Evaluation of Capacity to Confess, *Alan M. Goldstein and Naomi Goldstein*

Evaluation of Sexually Violent Predators, *Philip H. Witt and Mary Alice Conroy*

Evaluation for Risk of Violence in Adults, *Kirk Heilbrun*

Jury Selection, *Margaret Bull Kovera and Brian L. Cutler*

Evaluation for Capital Sentencing, *Mark D. Cunningham*

Eyewitness Identification, *Brian L. Cutler and Margaret Bull Kovera*

Civil Titles

Evaluation of Capacity to Consent to Treatment and Research, *Scott Y. H. Kim*

Evaluation for Guardianship, *Eric Y. Drogin and Curtis L. Barrett*

Evaluation for Personal Injury Claims, *Andrew W. Kane and Joel Dvoskin*

Evaluation for Civil Commitment, *Debra Pinals and Douglas Mossman*

Evaluation for Harassment and Discrimination Claims, *William Foote and Jane Goodman-Delahunty*

Evaluation of Workplace Disability, *Lisa D. Piechowski*

Juvenile and Family Titles

Evaluation for Child Custody, *Geri S.W. Fuhrmann*

Evaluation of Juveniles' Competence to Stand Trial, *Ivan Kruh and Thomas Grisso*

Evaluation for Risk of Violence in Juveniles, *Robert Hoge and D.A. Andrews*

Evaluation for Child Protection, *Karen S. Budd, Jennifer Clark, Mary Connell, and Kathryn Kuehnle*

Evaluation for Disposition and Transfer of Juvenile Offenders, *Randall T. Salekin*

EVALUATION FOR RISK OF VIOLENCE IN JUVENILES

ROBERT D. HOGE

AND D. A. ANDREWS

OXFORD
UNIVERSITY PRESS

2010

OXFORD
UNIVERSITY PRESS

Oxford University Press, Inc., publishes works that further
Oxford University's objective of excellence
in research, scholarship, and education.

Oxford   New York
Auckland   Cape Town   Dar es Salaam   Hong Kong   Karachi
Kuala Lumpur   Madrid   Melbourne   Mexico City   Nairobi
New Delhi   Shanghai   Taipei   Toronto

With offices in
Argentina   Austria   Brazil   Chile   Czech Republic   France   Greece
Guatemala   Hungary   Italy   Japan   Poland   Portugal   Singapore
South Korea   Switzerland   Thailand   Turkey   Ukraine   Vietnam

Published by Oxford University Press, Inc.
198 Madison Avenue, New York, New York 10016

www.oup.com

Oxford is a registered trademark of Oxford University Press

Library of Congress Cataloging-in-Publication Data
CIP data on file
ISBN 978-0-19-537041-6

9 8 7 6 5 4 3 2 1

About Best Practices in Forensic Mental Health Assessment

The recent growth in the fields of forensic psychology and forensic psychiatry has created a need for this book series describing best practices in forensic mental health assessment (FMHA). Currently, forensic evaluations are conducted by mental health professionals for a variety of criminal, civil, and juvenile legal questions. The research foundation supporting these assessments has become broader and deeper in recent decades. Consensus has become clearer on the recognition of essential requirements for ethical and professional conduct. In the larger context of the current emphasis on "empirically supported" assessment and intervention in psychiatry and psychology, the specialization of FMHA has advanced sufficiently to justify a series devoted to best practices. Although this series focuses mainly on evaluations conducted by psychologists and psychiatrists, the fundamentals and principles offered also apply to evaluations conducted by clinical social workers, psychiatric nurses, and other mental health professionals.

This series describes "best practice" as empirically supported (when the relevant research is available), legally relevant, and consistent with applicable ethical and professional standards. Authors of the books in this series identify the approaches that seem best, while incorporating what is practical and acknowledging that best practice represents a goal to which the forensic clinician should aspire, rather than a standard that can always be met. The American Academy of Forensic Psychology assisted the editors in enlisting the consultation of board-certified forensic psychologists specialized in each topic area. Board-certified forensic psychiatrists were also consultants on many of the volumes. Their comments on the manuscripts helped to ensure that the methods described in these volumes represent a generally accepted view of best practice.

The series' authors were selected for their specific expertise in a particular area. At the broadest level, however, certain general principles apply to all types of forensic evaluations. Rather than repeat those fundamental principles in every volume, the series offers them in the first volume, *Foundations of Forensic Mental Health Assessment*. Reading the first book, followed by a specific topical book, will provide the reader both the general principles that the specific topic shares with all forensic evaluations and those that are particular to the specific assessment question.

The specific topics of the 19 books were selected by the series editors as the most important and oft-considered areas of forensic assessment conducted by mental health professionals and behavioral scientists. Each of the 19 topical books is organized according to a common template. The authors address the applicable legal context, forensic mental health concepts, and empirical foundations and limits in the "Foundation" part of the book. They then describe preparation for the evaluation, data collection, data interpretation, and report writing and testimony in the "Application" part of the book. This creates a fairly uniform approach to considering these areas across different topics. All authors in this series have attempted to be as concise as possible in addressing best practice in their area. In addition, topical volumes feature elements to make them user friendly in actual practice. These elements include boxes that highlight especially important information, relevant case law, best-practice guidelines, and cautions against common pitfalls. A glossary of key terms is also provided in each volume.

We hope the series will be useful for different groups of individuals. Practicing forensic clinicians will find succinct, current information relevant to their practice. Those who are in training to specialize in FMHA (whether in formal training or in the process of respecialization) should find helpful the combination of broadly applicable considerations presented in the first volume together with the more specific aspects of other volumes in the series. Those who teach and supervise trainees can offer these volumes as a guide for practices to which the trainee can aspire. Researchers and scholars interested in FMHA best practice may find researchable ideas, particularly on topics that have received insufficient research attention to date. Judges and attorneys with questions about FMHA best practice will find these books relevant and concise. Clinical and forensic administrators who run agencies, court clinics, and hospitals in which litigants are assessed may also use some of the books in this series to establish expectancies for evaluations performed by professionals in their agencies.

We also anticipate that the 19 specific books in this series will serve as reference works that help courts and attorneys evaluate the quality of forensic mental health professionals' evaluations. A word of caution is in order, however. These volumes focus on best practice, not what is minimally acceptable legally or ethically. Courts involved in malpractice litigation, or ethics committees or licensure boards considering complaints, should not expect that materials describing best practice easily or necessarily translate into the minimally acceptable professional conduct that is typically at issue in such proceedings.

This book describes the important developments in violence risk assessment with juveniles, particularly over the last two decades. It does not address risk assessment with either adults or sexual offenders, as both are described in other books in this series. It does place juvenile risk assessment within the context of FMHA for juveniles, so those using it will find it particularly useful to incorporate into their evaluations of risk and needs for adolescents in the juvenile justice system.

Kirk Heilbrun
Thomas Grisso
Alan M. Goldstein

Acknowledgements

The authors wish to thank the following for their editorial advice and support: Kirk Heilbrun, Thomas Grisso, Randy Borum, and Julia TerMaat. Their help has been invaluable in the preparation of this book.

Contents

FOUNDATION

The Legal Context | 1

T he goal of this volume is to provide guidelines for the assessment and management of violent actions on the part of adolescents. This involves, first, formulating rules and procedures for identifying and measuring individual and circumstantial factors predisposing a youth to engage in aggressive actions. This is the risk assessment part of the task. Second, once the factors associated with increased risk for violence are identified, interventions to reduce the level of risk can be developed. This is the case management part of the task. This volume addresses these goals and references recent psychological and criminological research on juvenile criminal activity.

Chapter 2 provides a discussion of the various forms of violent acts, but it should be acknowledged here that a wide range of actions can be subsumed under this label. The acts can vary in terms of context, motivation, and severity of consequences. A school-yard fist fight and an act of violence conducted during a sexual assault constitute very different challenges for risk assessment and management as we will see in subsequent discussions.

This chapter is designed to discuss the larger legal and social contexts within which violence risk and management assessments are conducted. The discussion is based on a recognition of the absence of case law directly relevant to the judicial treatment of the young offender. It begins with background information, an introduction to alternative models of juvenile justice, and a brief discussion of juvenile justice systems in the United States. This is followed by discussions of rates and prevalence of violent crime and of public perceptions of violent youth crime. The various decision areas encountered in juvenile justice systems are reviewed, along with information about the role of risks and needs assessments in those decisions. Finally, a review of principles of best practice is presented as background to case planning and management of violent youth.

Background Information

Prediction and Management

Heilbrun (1997) distinguishes between two goals within the legal decision-making context: *prediction* and *risk management*. Prediction refers to providing estimates of the likelihood that the individual will engage in a particular action in the future. In the present case the concern is with estimating a youth's chances of committing an act of violence in the future. Prediction is important for a range of forensic decisions, including civil commitment, waivers to the adult criminal system, pretrial detention, and sentencing. In all of those cases the court may be seeking guidance on the probability of a future act of aggression.

Management decisions are directed toward the reduction of risk factors. In this case the concern is not only with formulating a prediction about future behavior but also with identifying risk factors that can be altered to reduce the probability of committing a violent act. Information pertaining to case management is relevant where the judicial system will have continued contact with the youth through, for example, probation or custody, and where intervention services can be offered.

As Heilbrun indicates, prediction and management decisions are closely related to one another. However, the management process is more dynamic than that of prediction because the concern is with changes over time. Further, reporting information about case planning and management is different in the sense that it requires a broader range of information about the youth than does prediction. The latter simply requires some estimate of the likelihood of reoffending.

INFO

The two goals of legal decision making are

- prediction of future violence
- management of risk factors

Risk/Needs Model

The terminology of this volume will follow a Risk/Needs model

INFO

Information relevant to case management includes

- dynamic risk factors
- responsivity factors
- protective or strength factors

of juvenile justice processing (Andrews & Bonta, 2006; Andrews, Bonta, & Hoge, 1990; Hoge & Andrews, 1996). *Risk assessment* refers to the collection and synthesis of information relevant to evaluating the youth's risk for antisocial actions. This forms the basis for risk predictions. *Needs assessment* refers to the collection and synthesis of information on *dynamic risk factors*, that is, risk factors that can be changed and, if changed, that will reduce the likelihood of antisocial actions. Examples include negative peer associations, impulsivity, and antisocial attitudes and values. Needs assessment forms the basis for case management decisions.

Responsivity and Strength

The constructs of *responsivity* and *strength* are also relevant for management decision making. The concept of responsivity includes factors referring to the characteristics of the youth or her circumstances that, though not directly related to the criminal activity, should be taken into account in case planning. Examples include readiness for treatment, reading ability, or a mood disorder. The construct also includes the rule that modes and strategies of service offered the youth should match the characteristics of the youth. Protective or strength factors refer to variables that may serve to ameliorate the effects of risk. Examples include a mature personality, interest in a sport, or a cooperative parent. These factors are relevant to case planning and management as well.

Alternative Models of Juvenile Justice

Table 1.1 presents an outline of five models for describing juvenile justice systems. All models espouse the same goal: the

Table 1.1 | Models of Juvenile Justice

Child Welfare
Focus on developing competencies in the youth and addressing situational problems; services delivered in judicial system with cooperation of external educational, mental health, and social services; de-emphasis of punitive sanctions in favor of rehabilitative efforts.
Corporatist
Focus on diversion from juvenile justice system and providing rehabilitative services through the educational, mental health, and social service systems.
Justice
Emphasis on the processing of the youth within a judicial system with primary concern for protecting individual rights and insuring that legally mandated procedures are observed; some concern for rehabilitation but focus generally on promoting individual responsibility through the use of punitive correctional sanctions.
Modified Justice
Rehabilitative and punitive services delivered through the juvenile justice system; emphasis on formal judicial processing; effort to achieve a balance between rehabilitative and punitive strategies.
Crime Control
Focus on providing protection to society through the use of punitive sanctions; primary concern with offense rather than offender; punitive sanctions preferred, with the sanction often based on retributive or just deserts considerations.
Note. From Corrado, R. R. (1992). Introduction. In R. R. Corrado, N. Bala, R. Linden, & M. Le Blanc (Eds.), *Juvenile justice in Canada: A theoretical and analytical assessment* (pp. 1–20). Toronto: Butterworth.

deterrence of criminal actions on the part of youth. However, the models differ in assumptions about the optimal means for achieving that goal and consequently the preferred procedures for the processing and treatment of the youthful offender. The models can be represented on a continuum

INFO

Models of juvenile justice vary in their focus, some more focused on enhancing the competencies of the youth and others more focused on responding to the criminal act.

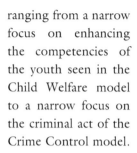

ranging from a narrow focus on enhancing the competencies of the youth seen in the Child Welfare model to a narrow focus on the criminal act of the Crime Control model.

1
chapter

Child Welfare Model

The fundamental assumption of this model is that antisocial behavior of the young person can be addressed best by enhancing his behavioral and emotional competencies and by addressing the deficits in his environment. These goals can be achieved by providing appropriate therapeutic, counseling, and educational services to youth and parents. This model is applied within a formal juvenile justice system, but in this case there is less emphasis on legal processing and more on providing rehabilitative interventions. The system often reflects a *parens patriae* concept whereby the state reserves a right to assume responsibility for the well-being of the young person.

Legal sanctioning and punishment generally play a smaller role in systems guided by child welfare concerns than those located closer to the crime control end of the continuum. Rather, the emphasis is on rehabilitative interventions provided by medical, social work, or mental health professionals. Judicial and correctional workers too are expected to focus on child welfare and rehabilitative goals. It is difficult to identify pure applications of the Child Welfare model; however, many systems in the United States, Canada, and elsewhere that are described as reflecting a Modified Justice model incorporate features of the Child Welfare model to some degree.

Corporatist Model

This model is described by Corrado (1992) and Pratt (1989) as a variation on the Child Welfare model. The model shares with the latter an emphasis on interventions aimed at addressing specific deficits in the youth and her environment, but departs from the

Child Welfare model by emphasizing the importance of integrating services for children into a single system of care. The keys to the model are the diversion of youth from the formal justice system and an integration of services for them. Ideally, the services should be provided in a single system offering mental health, educational, and counseling services to youth and their families.

The Corporatist model represents an ideal for those embracing a child welfare and rehabilitation orientation and for those who are critical of the fragmented system of youth and family services seen in many jurisdictions. It is difficult to find examples of the Corporatist model, but the Scottish system at least approximates the model. Although provisions exist in this system for diverting youth who have committed a very serious crime to the criminal justice system, the majority of youth who have committed criminal acts are dealt with in an integrated juvenile justice, mental health, education, and social service system.

Justice Model

The focus in this model shifts from a concern for the needs of the individual offender toward the criminal act and the appropriate legal responses to that act. The principal goals in this case are to ensure that the civil rights of the youth are protected, that prescribed legal procedures are observed, and that a disposition appropriate to the crime is achieved. The Justice model is generally considered antithetical to a *parens patriae* orientation.

Juvenile justice systems reflecting this orientation vary somewhat in terms of legal processing procedures, but the major source of variation probably concerns sanctioning procedures. Whether individual deterrence, group deterrence, or punishment should be the primary purpose of sentencing is often debated. Similarly, there is always a debate in this type of system over the extent to which diversion, probation, or custody sanctions should be employed. Rehabilitative efforts play only a minor role in these systems.

Modified Justice Model

This model combines elements of both the Child Welfare and Justice models. It reflects a child welfare orientation by recognizing that the control of youth crime depends ultimately on providing young people with the resources to lead a prosocial lifestyle, and that this is best achieved through the provision of prevention and intervention programs. On the other hand, these rehabilitation efforts are delivered in the context of a legal system with its concerns for legal rights and judicial processing.

There is clearly an inherent tension within this model concerning the relative emphasis placed on the child welfare and judicial processing components. There may also be pressure in this type of model toward the crime control end of the continuum, with its concern for immediate measures to control crime. These kinds of pressures are often observed in political debates about the best approach for dealing with youthful criminal activity (Feld, 1999; Schwartz, 1992).

Crime Control Model

This model shares with the Justice model a dependence on formal legal processing procedures. However, though the focus in the Justice model is on legal rights and procedures, the primary concern in this model is with the use of legal sanctions against offenders to ensure protection of society. There is, then, less concern with the individual offender in this model than in any of the other models.

Both this and the preceding model derive largely from the *Classical Theory of Crime*. Criminal acts are viewed as willful, representing moral transgressions. The only appropriate responses to these acts are criminal sanctions, preferably involving incarceration. Although more minor cases might be dealt with through diversion procedures, there is generally little concern with rehabilitation efforts in this approach.

Juvenile Justice Systems in the United States

Judicial decisions of the federal courts impose some guidelines on the treatment of juvenile offenders in the United States. However, primary responsibility for youth who engage in criminal activities rests with the state governments. They are responsible for formulating laws and policies and for the processing of youth who come into conflict with the law. Historical treatments show that systems for dealing with youth crime have evolved slowly since the first juvenile court was created in Chicago in 1899.

States show considerable variability in juvenile justice laws and practices, but the majority of the systems reflect a Justice or Modified Justice model. In most cases there are legal guidelines regarding the processing of the offender, including safeguards to protect the rights of the young person. In most jurisdictions, some efforts to address the risks and needs factors of the youth are present. The tension within these systems, and the factor contributing most to variability among the state systems, concerns the relative emphasis placed on a rehabilitative versus punitive focus. All systems contain both elements, but some place considerably more emphasis on diversion and rehabilitation than do others. It is safe to say that no system in the United States reflects a pure Child Welfare, Corporatist, or Crime model, although some very punitive systems may approach the Crime model (Feld, 1999; Schwartz, 1992).

Rate and Prevalence of Juvenile Violent Crime

Though the public, politicians, and the media all have opinions about the incidence of violent actions on the part of youth, establishing objective data is problematic (Barkan, 2006; Loeber, Farrington, & Waschbush, 1998; Snyder & Sickmund, 1999; Williams, Tuthill, & Lo, 2008). Two types of data are reported regarding incidence: *rates* and *prevalence*.

Rates

Rates refer to the incidence of the activities within a particular time frame, area, or sample. This might involve, for example, data about the numbers of murders, auto thefts, or robberies committed by young people in a community over a 1-year period. These data are often expressed in relative terms, where, for example, the number of murder convictions are expressed as 6 per 100,000 individuals within the population of interest. A particular concern is often with rates of violent crimes over time, that is, with whether crime rates are increasing or decreasing.

INFO

Typical data sources for rates and prevalence of juvenile criminal activity include

- self-report surveys
- victim surveys
- official statistics

Prevalence

The second type of information reflects the prevalence of criminal activity among youth. Whereas incidence figures are based on the number of incidents or cases of crimes, prevalence rates are based on the number of youth committing crimes. Prevalence indices are usually expressed in percentage terms. For example, we may be interested in comparing the percentages of boys and girls convicted of juvenile offenses or in contrasting samples of youth drawn from inner city and suburban areas in terms of the frequency of arrests for violent offenses.

Sources

Data for determining both rates and prevalence generally derive from one of three sources: self-report surveys, victim surveys, and official statistics. However, all of these sources are limited in some respects. Self-report surveys are dependent on the sample of respondents and the honesty of the respondents. Victim surveys probably provide underestimates of rates and incidence because, for whatever reason, many victims do not report crimes.

In a sense official records represent the most objective source of information regarding criminal activity. They are based on records of the actual incidence of criminal arrests, charges, or convictions. Table 1.2 lists the major sources of official records.

However, these data also suffer from some limitations. First, they are based on official judicial processing and, hence, count only cases where the youth is apprehended for the crime and processing is carried out in the system. For this reason, the official figures likely underestimate the true extent of antisocial activity. Second, the data are

BEWARE
Official records may not give an accurate or complete picture of a youth's antisocial activity.

Table 1.2 | Sources of Official Statistics on Juvenile Offending

Juvenile Court Statistics Report—Office of Juvenile Justice and Delinquency Prevention
Juvenile Offenders and Victims—Office of Juvenile Justice and Delinquency Prevention
National Juvenile Court Data Archive—Office of Juvenile Justice and Delinquency
Prevention
Sourcebook of Criminal Justice Statistics—Hindelang Criminal Justice Research Center
Uniform Crime Report—Federal Bureau of Investigation
Youth Risk Behavior Survey—Centers for Disease Control and Prevention

dependent on the quality of record keeping and reporting by juvenile justice agencies, and problems may exist in this respect.

Conclusions

In spite of these measurement problems, it is possible to derive some conclusions regarding the incidence of violent actions among youth (see Blumstein, Farrington, & Moitra, 1985; Krisberg, Hartney, Wolf, & Silva, 2009; Loeber et al., 1998; Williams et al., 2008). The major trends may be summarized as follows:

- The majority of youth are basically responsible and law-abiding citizens, although risk taking and engagement in minor criminal transgressions (e.g., underage drinking, vandalism) are normative among adolescents; further, a significant percentage of male and female adolescents engage in some forms of minor violent actions, although the actions are generally not serious enough to come to the attention of the justice system.

- A small percentage of youth engage in violent actions serious enough to merit the attention of the police and the justice system; most of these activities are relatively minor and in the majority of cases the youth do not engage in continued criminal activity.

- An even smaller percentage of youth commit serious violent actions that merit judicial intervention; however, in the majority of these cases the youth do not continue to engage in serious criminal actions.
- A small minority of youth begin criminal careers early, escalate the seriousness of criminal activities in adolescence, and persist in these activities into the adult years; some of these youth engage in serious violent crimes.

The last group is very important and will be discussed further in later chapters.

The pattern of violent offending has changed over time. Between 1980 and 1984 there was a significant increase in the number of youth arrested for both lethal and nonlethal violent crimes. However, since 1984 the rate of juvenile violent crime has shown a decline, with the decline being particularly sharp between 1992 and 2003. This decline is for both Caucasian and African American males, although some data show increases in violent actions on the part of female adolescents (Pepler & Craig, 2005). A decline in violent actions is also reflected in data collected from school settings (National Center for Education Statistics, 2006).

Explanations for the decline in violent acts on the part of male youth are complex, involving changes in population demographics, economic conditions, and juvenile justice system responses to youth crime.

It is difficult to analyze how racial differences contribute to crime. Data from both official and self-report sources indicate higher levels of criminal activity among African American males than among Caucasian males, although the differences are smaller when examining self-report data. The recorded rates of violent crime are particularly high for African American males as compared to other groups. However, interpreting these differences is difficult and involves questions of socioeconomic status, neighborhood conditions, and the operation of racial bias in the police and juvenile justice systems (Cernkovich, Giodarno, & Rudolph, 2000; Williams, Ayers, Outlaw, Abbott, & Hawkins, 2001).

The fact that only a small percentage of youth engage in serious violent criminal activity and that rates of juvenile violent crime have not increased over the past 25 or so years should be kept in mind when there is talk of making the juvenile justice system more stringent. On the other hand, some youth continue to engage in violent actions and this remains a cause for concern.

Public Perceptions of Violent Youth Crime

Opinion surveys nearly always show that the public perceives crime to be a significant social issue, that their communities are not safe, and that crime rates, particularly rates of serious violent crime, are increasing nationally and locally (Warr, 2007). These opinions are often accompanied by a demand for more punitive action for offenders. The surveys also reveal that violent crime is perceived to be a threat in the school setting, with schools being considered as more dangerous places than in the past (Maguire & Pastore, 1995). Although questions have been raised about the methodology of this opinion research (Warr, 2007), these attitudes and perceptions exist and are capable of affecting public policy.

Accuracy of Perception

The key question concerns the extent to which these public perceptions reflect reality. Expert analyses conducted by Elliott, Hamburg, and Williams (1998), Krisberg et al. (2009), Maguire and Pastore (1996), Schwartz (1992), Warr (2007), Zimring (1998), and others clearly demonstrate that public perceptions are not accurate and reflect exaggerated fears of crime, particularly violent crime.

Two sources of these exaggerated fears can be identified. The media have often been implicated

INFO

Public perception often overestimates rates of crime, but nonetheless influences public policy.

in promoting an exaggerated fear of crime by emphasizing and sometimes romanticizing crime and criminals (Surette, 1992; Warr, 2007). The influence of the media operates through news reports that focus on dramatic but rare acts of violence (e.g., school shootings) and through TV, film, or video game content displaying extreme acts of violence. Second, political leaders are sometimes accused of exaggerating the incidence of crime for political ends.

Impact on Public Policy

Whatever the accuracy of public perceptions of violent youth crime, those perceptions are very important from the point of view of guiding public policy regarding the treatment of youthful offending. The danger is that, where the perceptions are inaccurate, inappropriate strategies may be employed in responding to youth crime.

Decision Contexts for Risk and Management Assessments

Assessments of propensity for violence are conducted in a variety of settings. Schools are particularly concerned with evaluating a student's risk for violence in order to ensure the protection of students and staff and to decide about appropriate interventions for the youth presenting the risk. Clinicians in mental health institutions and community settings are often called on to provide risk assessments. The evaluations in these cases may be made to aid decisions about civil commitments, institutional placements, or appropriate treatment strategies.

The focus in this book is on the assessment and management of violence propensity in forensic settings. Figure 1.1 lists the major decision areas represented in juvenile justice systems. The role of violence risk and management assessments will be discussed as they occur in each decision area.

Precharge Level

A variety of options are available at the precharge level. The first, and a very common action, is a police decision to simply dismiss the case, with or without a warning or notice to the parent. This is generally based on the severity of the offense and a very informal assessment of risk on the part of the police officer.

Some juvenile justice systems include a diversion provision whereby the youth is not charged with an offense but, rather, is directed toward an intervention program of some sort. Generally, these programs involve an accountability component whereby the youth admits to the transgression and possibly engages in some sort of compensatory activity. The diversion program may also involve directing the youth toward a treatment intervention designed to address factors placing the youth at risk. Successful completion of these programs generally terminate involvement with the system.

The decision to divert the youth may rest with police, prosecutors, or, in some jurisdictions, intake probation officers. In fact, some agencies have developed systematic assessment procedures for identifying youth eligible for diversion programs. The programs are usually designed for youth who have committed relatively minor crimes. Risk assessments are involved in the diversion decisions because youth at high risk for continued criminal activity, particularly violent actions, would generally not qualify for the programs, although well-resourced programs may make exceptions (Altschuler, 1998). When the youth is accepted to the diversion program, a risk/needs assessment is required to decide what kinds of intervention programs might be required. In many cases the risks and needs assessments are made in an informal manner by judicial personnel with no particular training in the conduct of assessments. In other cases, however, structured assessment procedures are introduced for case planning and management in the diversion program.

Postcharge/Preadjudication

A number of decisions involving risk assessments may be required after a charge has been filed but before the formal adjudication process begins. Some of these such as waiver of *Miranda* rights, transfer to the adult system, or competence to stand trial generally involve assessments of risk for violence and a full mental health assessment (see Grisso, 1998, 2004, 2005a). Decisions regarding preadjudication detention and preadjudication diversion may require assessments of risks and needs.

PREADJUDICATION DETENTION

Judgments about risk for engaging in criminal activities, particularly violent actions, are often the major basis for a decision to detain the youth in custody before further processing. These risk assessments are generally made in an informal and unsystematic manner by police or prosecutors. The issue of case management often does not arise in detention decisions because preadjudication periods are generally of short duration and because programming might conflict with the individual's legal rights.

PREADJUDICATION DIVERSION

Some juvenile justice systems have alternative measures or provisions whereby a youth will voluntarily enter a treatment program of some sort before being subjected to further judicial processing. Successful completion of the program generally ends the judicial processing (either through a dismissal of charges or by a conditional discharge). Both risk and management assessments are relevant to alternative measures programs. Often a youth at high risk for a violent action will not be considered suitable for such a program. However, once a youth has been accepted, an assessment of his criminogenic needs is required to guide decisions about appropriate programming. In well-designed programs, these risks and needs assessments are conducted in a structured manner.

Adjudication

Neither risk assessment nor risk management decisions should play a role in the adjudication process. Findings of innocence or guilt are based solely on the circumstances of the case.

Disposition

It is at the disposition phase that risks and needs assessments become important, although their role sometimes raises difficult legal and

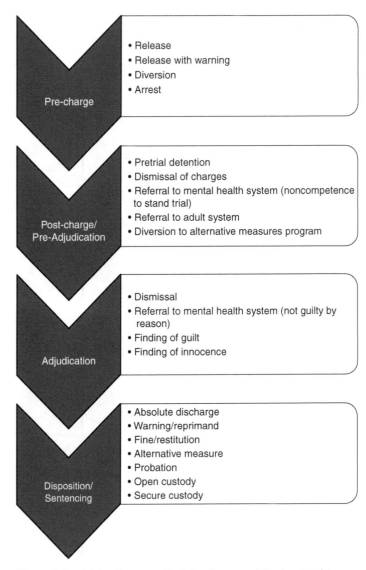

Figure 1.1   Major Statutory Decision Areas and Options Within Juvenile Justice Systems

ethical issues. The various disposition and sanctioning options available to the juvenile court have been outlined in Figure 1.1.

The choice of a sanction following a finding of guilt, whether probation, some form of incarceration, or other option, represents the initial choice. Second, a decision must generally be made regarding the terms of the disposition. The latter might involve, for example, setting the length of a term of custody or the level of probation supervision. Within most systems in the United States these decisions are made by a judge.

Some have argued that allowing assessments of risk for general or violent offending or reoffending to influence disposition decisions may represent a threat to the legal rights of the offender. Should two youth who have committed the same offense and with the same history of offending be given different sentences because one is at higher risk to reoffend than the other? There could be two objections to this. The first argument flows from the *just deserts* position that the only justifiable basis for sentencing concerns the nature and severity of the crime committed. Any other consideration is irrelevant. The second argument states that our ability to form risk predictions is imperfect, and, therefore, these should not be the basis for sentencing decisions. This issue will be explored further in later chapters.

However, whatever position is taken regarding the role of risk assessments in the initial sentencing decision, it is clear that risks and needs assessment can play a useful role in case planning and management once that decision has been made. These can help guide whatever intervention is to be provided within the disposition.

PROBATION

A period of mandatory supervision by a probation or parole officer in the community is the most common disposition employed in juvenile justice systems. Risks and needs assessments can help to guide this process in two ways. First, the level or closeness of supervision should be guided, in part, by the level of risk presented by the youth. Those at higher levels of risk for continued criminal activity, particularly violent activity, would require closer community supervision than those at lower risk. Second, the risk/needs assessment can provide guidance in planning therapeutic or other interventions appropriate for the youth.

INCARCERATION/CUSTODY

A sentence of confinement to a custodial institution is a very common disposition in juvenile justice systems. Risks and needs assessments can play a role similar to that of probation. The level of security afforded the youth will depend to some extent on his risk for committing another offense, particularly an act of violence. Second, programming within the institution should be guided by a careful assessment of the treatment needs of the youth.

Unfortunately, risks and needs assessments for offering guidance in probation and custody settings are often conducted through unstructured and informal procedures. These procedures often present a distorted picture of the youth and lead to poor decisions regarding the youth's treatment.

Research-Based Principles of Best Practice

This volume is concerned with developing guidelines for evaluating a youth's risk for violence and with developing case planning and management strategies for addressing the risk factors, thereby reducing the probability that the youth will continue to engage in antisocial actions. This section, derived from research literature, presents a review of principles of best practice in the treatment of youthful offenders.

A growing body of research from program evaluation studies is providing important guidance regarding the kinds of procedures most likely to address the problems of the juvenile offender. It is also worth noting that the quality of this research is constantly improving, and,

BEST PRACTICE

Features of Effective Programming

- Use standardized assessment procedures
- Observe the risk principle
- Observe the need principle
- Observe the responsivity principle
- Take account of protective or strength factors
- Utilize community-based interventions
- Address needs in the institutional setting
- Deliver multimodal services
- Offer structured programs with concrete behavioral goals
- Offer aftercare services following institutional treatment
- Monitor program delivery and impact

hence, confidence in the conclusions is growing. Reviews of the research literature on effective programming have been provided by Andrews and Bonta (2006), Guerra, Kim, and Boxer (2008b), Heilbrun, Lee, and Cottle (2005), Krisberg and Howell (1998), Lipsey (1995, 2006), and Lipsey and Wilson (1998). The following is a review of the features of effective programming emerging from that research:

Standardized Assessment Procedures

Research cited in the reviews cited above demonstrate that programs using structured and standardized assessment procedures are more effective in reducing reoffending than those depending on purely clinical or informal assessment procedures. This issue will be discussed further in later chapters.

The Risk Principle

The risk principle of case classification states that higher-risk cases should be provided with intensive intervention services, whereas lower-risk cases can be provided less intensive services. For example, in the case of probation, close and intensive monitoring can be reserved for those at greatest risk for continuing antisocial behavior. Similarly, lengthy and expensive treatment programs should involve those with high levels of need. This principle is important for a number of reasons. First, most systems have limited resources and these should not be wasted on youth who do not really require the services. Second, overinvolvement of lower-risk youth in the system may have negative consequences (see Dishion, McCord, & Poulin, 1999; Dodge, Dishion, & Lansford, 2006). This is illustrated where low-risk youth incarcerated with high-risk youth begin to show increased levels of risk.

The Need Principle

The need principle of case classification states that programs should target the specific needs of the youth; that is, they should focus on eliminating or ameliorating those factors that place the youth at risk for antisocial behavior. If the

BEWARE
Low-risk youth may be negatively influenced by association with higher-risk youth.

youth's delinquency relates to inadequate parenting and associations with antisocial peers, then interventions should focus on those specific areas of need. Two considerations underlie this principle. First, by observing the principle maximum use is made of limited resources. Second, research discussed in the reviews and meta-analyses cited above demonstrates that interventions have their greatest impact when they focus on the needs of the individual. Unfortunately, many juvenile justice systems are rigid in the programming and do not permit the necessary levels of individualization.

The Responsivity Principle

The responsivity principle states that case planning should recognize characteristics or circumstances of the youth that are not directly related to their criminal activity and then take them into account in case planning. For example, there is little point in placing a youth with limited reading skills in a cognitive behavior modification program requiring the reading of complicated material. Another illustration would involve a girl whose criminal activities are clearly associated with her associations with an antisocial group of youth and drug abuse. However, she may also be suffering from depression and anxiety associated with past abuse, and those conditions would have to be taken into account in planning an intervention.

Protective or Strength Factors

Case plans should be built to the extent possible on the strengths of the youth or his circumstances. For example, if cooperative parents are available, they should certainly be involved in the intervention. Similarly, a risk related to poor use of leisure time could be addressed where the youth has an interest in a particular sport.

Community-Based Interventions

Research demonstrates that delivering interventions to the offender in her community setting is more effective than intervening in institutional settings. This is not

BEWARE
The success of community-based efforts depends on the availability of quality services in the community.

surprising. The young person's risk for criminal activities relates to conditions at home, in the neighborhood, and at school, and efforts to address those conditions are best undertaken in those settings.

Needs in the Institutional Setting

Research demonstrates that, where institutionalization or incarceration is necessary, success depends on providing interventions that address the needs of the youth. Simply incarcerating youth without any efforts to address behavioral, emotional, social, or educational needs does not reduce reoffending rates. In fact, it often has the opposite effect of increasing anger and a sense of alienation.

Multimodal Services

Effective programs address the entire range of interacting problems presented by the client. Youths do not come to the juvenile justice system with isolated issues. Instead, they often present to us a range of connected risk and need factors, and interventions that address the set of needs are more effective than those that have a narrow focus. This is why, for example, placing a youth in a substance abuse program without acknowledging that the problem is linked with supervision problems in his home, an association with a substance-abusing friend, and frustration with school failure will not be very successful.

Structured Programs With Concrete Behavioral Goals

The efficacy of juvenile offender interventions that are highly structured and directed toward altering specific behavioral and attitudinal deficits in the youth is strongly supported by research. The most effective goals entail social problem-solving and decision skills, moral reasoning, and the development of prosocial attitudes, values, and beliefs. Programs based on behavior modification, cognitive-behavioral, and skill training procedures are particularly effective.

Aftercare Services Following Institutional Treatment

Effective programs provide continuing services to the youth after release from custody or other institutional settings. This is essential to ensure that any gains made in the institution transfer to the youth's home, community, and school environment. Release planning should be an important part of any residential program.

Program Delivery and Impact

Effective programs have in place formal procedures for describing and evaluating service delivery (process evaluation) and program impact (summative evaluation). An expanding body of research demonstrates that the effectiveness of interventions depends very directly on the care with which programs are delivered. Ideally, evaluation efforts should be undertaken internally and externally. Independent external evaluations are particularly important.

INFO

Evidence Based Programs

The principles discussed in this section represent general guidelines for program development. It is also worth noting that a limited number of evidence-based programs have been identified (Guerra et al., 2008b; Lipsey, 2006; Lipsey & Wilson, 1998; Tolan & Guerra, 1994). Examples of programs for which strong research support is available include Multisystemic Therapy, Aggression Replacement Training, and Functional Family Therapy. However, two points must be kept in mind in applying these programs. First, the effectiveness of these programs has not been evaluated for all types of youth or for all situations. Second, it is important to remember that effective implementation of the programs is critical to their success.

Forensic Mental Health Concepts | **2**

I dentification of the violent juvenile offender requires definitions of violent acts and criminal acts. Simply describing a
youth as having committed a violent act or at risk for doing so
does not provide a clear understanding about the youth. Efforts
to define violent and criminal acts will first be presented, followed
by alternative systems for describing youth who engage in serious
antisocial activities.

Defining Violent Criminal Actions

Aggressive conduct is defined in the Diagnostic and Statistical
Manual of Mental Disorders-IV—TR (DSM-IV-TR) as conduct
that "causes or threatens physical harm to other people or animals
(e.g., bullying, threatening, or intimidating others)" (American
Psychiatric Association, 2000). This includes any action causing physical or psychological harm to another. The terms *aggressive act* and
violent act are often used interchangeably, although the latter is
sometimes reserved for more serious actions causing physical harm.

Tolan and Gorman-Smith (2002) and Vitaro and Brendgen
(2005) are among the analysts who have argued that acts of violence
need to be understood in terms of the motivation or intention behind
the act and its consequences. One would not want to equate the
situation where a youth in a fit of anger shoves another with the
case of a young person assaulting another to steal a pair of shoes.

Reactive Versus Proactive Aggression

One useful distinction to be drawn from this literature is between
reactive and *proactive* aggressive actions. The former includes acts of

violence motivated by anger in response to real or perceived threats. This is a very common form of aggression in adolescents, and we will see that many youth with a high propensity for violence, the primary concern of this volume, engage in this form of aggression. Proactive aggression, on the other hand, is goal directed and motivated by a perception that the action will lead to a desirable reward. The young person who assaults another to steal drugs exhibits this form of aggression.

Tolan's Categories of Violent Acts

A somewhat different, although overlapping, categorization of violent acts has been proposed by Tolan (2007; Tolan and Guerra, 1994). The forms of aggression are labeled situational, relationship, predatory, and pathological.

SITUATIONAL

Situational acts of violence generally arise in response to social or contextual factors. This would include aggressive acts carried out in association with a group of peers or in response to contextual factors such as extreme provocation. The violent actions in this case are provoked by specific situational factors, although an underlying predisposition to violence may be present.

RELATIONSHIP

Relationship violence occurs within social relationships, such as between family members or in dating situations. The act of violence may arise from frustrations experienced in the relationship or may reflect predatory or pathological violence as described next.

PREDATORY

Predatory violence corresponds to the definition of instrumental aggression defined above. In this case the act of violence is committed in an effort to obtain a desired reward. Only a small number of adolescents exhibit a pattern of chronic predatory violence, although these tend to be the most serious offenders (Tolan & Gorman-Smith, 1998, 2002).

PATHOLOGICAL

Finally, pathological violence appears in the apparent absence of situational triggers. These actions do not necessarily appear in the context of relationships or as instrumental acts designed to achieving desired outcomes. In this case the violence appears to be an end in itself. Fortunately, this type aggression is considered rare among adolescents.

The forms of aggression discussed here are not mutually exclusive, and some youth with a history of aggressive actions show a propensity for more than one form. Still, from the point of view of understanding the violent actions of a youth, distinctions among forms of violence can be important.

Labeling Violent Actions: Significant Issues

Significant issues arise in labeling violent actions as criminal acts. Previous discussions have indicated that criminal codes applying to youth differ in different national settings and sometimes within countries. However, serious acts of aggression or violence are generally treated as criminal depending on the age of the youth. Still, issues exist in the labeling of violent acts as criminal.

Labeling a violent act as criminal generally depends on the motivation behind the action and the consequences of the act. An act of violence on the part of a severely developmentally delayed youth would probably not be labeled a criminal act, nor would an accidental action causing physical injury during a sporting event. Although the judicial system sometimes has difficulty dealing with issues of intent and motivation, they are generally considered relevant to labeling an action as criminal.

INFO

Relevant factors
in labeling violent acts are

- intent and motivation
- severity
- chronicity

The severity of an action is also a factor in labeling the action as criminal, although in practice judging severity is not always a simple matter (Loeber et al., 1998). For example, a complaint is occasionally made that systems sometimes overcriminalize minor physical confrontations between youth. In any case, whether or not a violent action is considered criminal ultimately depends on the judicial system.

The chronicity of criminal actions is also a consideration in judging whether an individual is labeled a serious offender (Loeber et al., 1998). However, this label can be problematic because any effort at using the "chronicity" label will be arbitrary (Blumstein et al., 1985; Le Blanc, 1998). How many offenses does the youth have to commit and over what length of time before we label him a chronic offender?

Descriptive Systems for Juvenile Offenders

Labeling a youth as a serious or violent offender because she has committed a serious or violent criminal act does not provide us with a great deal of information about the youth. Similarly, indicating that the youth is at high risk for committing a violent act is of questionable value in the absence of a rationale for the prediction. A more thorough understanding of the youth is required for effective risk prediction and management.

A number of diagnostic and descriptive systems have been developed over the years for juvenile offenders. Most of them have been developed for describing youth who engage in general criminal activity, but most are also capable of providing insight into the behavioral, personality, and circumstantial characteristics of youth who commit serious and violent criminal actions or who are at risk for doing so. It should be understood that the

INFO

Common categories of descriptive systems are

- Offense-based systems
- Clinically based systems
- Personality-based systems
- Behavior-based systems
- Risk-based systems

description of these systems overlaps to some extent the review of theoretical and research advances in the analysis of youth crime discussed in chapter 3.

Offense-Based Systems

Offense-based systems describe the youth in terms of pattern of antisocial activities. The simplest categorization distinguishes offenders and nonoffenders. More complex systems are based on the kind of antisocial activity engaged in: nonserious offender, serious offender, property crime offender, violent offender, sex offender, or drug offender. However, even this type of categorization presents problems. First, as discussed above, identifying acts as serious or violent is not always simple. Second, these are not homogenous categories. Placing a youth convicted of a simple assault and one who engaged in a violent assault in the same category is problematic. A similar type of issue arises with the label "sex offender." These offenses can range from inappropriate touching to violent sexual assaults. The concept of chronicity is sometimes used to refine the offense-based categorizations, but as noted above issues arise here as well.

Another type of problem with offense-based systems is that antisocial youth often engage in various types of antisocial actions (Farrington, 1994; Tolan, 2007; West & Farrington, 1977). This is particularly true for youth engaging in serious and violent criminal activity. These youth often participate in a range of criminal activities.

The pattern of antisocial actions over time is another basis for describing offenders. Research on this topic will be discussed in detail in chapter 3 where a variety of patterns have been identified. For example, a distinction is made between life-course-persistent offenders who begin antisocial activities in childhood and persist through adolescence and adulthood and adolescent-onset offenders whose criminal actions tend to be confined to adolescence. Again, however, we are dealing with categories that are not entirely homogenous regarding the nature of the offenses committed or the behavioral, personality, or circumstantial characteristics of the youth.

BEWARE
Offense-based categorizations are inadequate to describe youth.

INFO

Two DSM-IV-TR diagnoses particularly relevant to juvenile offenders are

● conduct disorder

● oppositional-defiant disorder

The focus of this volume will remain on the violent offender in spite of the various problems associated with offense-based categorizations. However, it must be recognized that additional constructs are needed to fully describe the young people of interest.

Clinically Based Systems

A second approach to describing youth who engage in serious and violent crime is based on the clinical experience of mental health professionals. The International Classification of Diseases—10 (ICD-10; World Health Organization, 1992) and the DSM-IV-TR (American Psychiatric Association, 2000) are the major clinical diagnostic systems relevant to youthful offenders. These systems are widely used in clinical and forensic contexts.

The DSM-IV-TR will be used to illustrate the application of this type of system to youth engaging in serious and violent criminal activities. Two diagnostic categories are particularly relevant to juvenile offenders: *conduct disorder* and *oppositional-defiant disorder*.

CONDUCT DISORDER

Youth diagnosed as conduct disordered exhibit a persistent pattern of antisocial behavior, including rule breaking and aggressive acts. Four categories of actions are associated with the diagnostic category:

- Aggressive conduct, including actions causing physical harm to humans and animals
- Nonaggressive conduct, including property damage, arson, and vandalism
- Deceitfulness, including acts of theft and fraud
- Serious rule violation, including truancy and running from home

The severity of conduct disorder depends on the number and seriousness of the transgressions. Most youth committing serious and violent crimes would receive a diagnosis of conduct disorder.

Further, most of the individuals exhibiting a persistent pattern of serious and violent crime through adolescence will have shown symptoms of conduct disorder from an early age. This is identified as childhood-onset conduct disorder.

A wide range of more specific maladaptive traits are also identified as associated with the conduct disorder diagnosis. These include lack of empathy and remorse, irritability, impulsivity, early onset of sexual behavior, and substance abuse. These too are characteristics often observed clinically in youth engaging in serious violent criminal activity.

OPPOSITIONAL-DEFIANT DISORDER

Oppositional-defiant disorder is the second DSM-IV-TR diagnostic category frequently applied to juvenile offenders. The symptoms in this case include a persistent pattern of negative and hostile behavior toward authority figures such as parents, teachers, police, or probation officers. These behaviors may or may not be accompanied by aggressive and destructive conduct disorders. Serious violent offenders often show an escalating pattern of oppositional and defiant behaviors from childhood through adolescence.

GENDER DIFFERENCES

The symptoms of conduct disorder and oppositional-defiant disorder are generally robust across cultural and gender groups. However, the symptoms are more commonly observed in boys. Also, the expression of the symptoms is more likely to take an externalizing form (e.g., fighting, property destruction) in boys, whereas girls more often display internalizing or relational forms (e. g., running away, prostitution, relational aggression).

LIMITATIONS AND BENEFITS OF DIAGNOSTIC CATEGORIES

These DSM-IV-TR diagnostic categories are important in both clinical and forensic contexts. In clinical settings they aid in understanding and communicating problematic behavior of youth. In forensic contexts DSM-IV-TR diagnoses can assist in decisions regarding competency to stand trial or waiver of *Miranda* rights. Under some circumstances DSM-IV-TR diagnoses have a legal basis (Grisso, 1998, 2004). Finally, the diagnoses may have value in

BEST PRACTICE

Be familiar with the use of DSM-IV-TR diagnoses and their limitations in forensic settings.

disposition decisions about placement, sentencing, and case management decisions.

It is also necessary to note a number of cautions in the use of these psychiatric diagnoses. First, the symptoms contained within these diagnoses do not necessarily constitute criminal actions, and it is not entirely clear the extent to which the diagnostic categories relate to criminal behavior. Second, the diagnoses present only a summary of a range of maladaptive behaviors and provide very little information about the etiology or dynamics of the condition being summarized. Simply diagnosing a youth as conduct disordered tells us very little about why these behaviors developed or the implications of the behaviors for future adjustment. Third, questions have been raised about the validity of the diagnostic categories and the reliability with which they are formed (Nathan & Langenbucher, 1999). Finally, DSM-IV-TR reflects a medical model and focuses almost exclusively on the individual, neglecting important environmental factors affecting the individual.

Personality-Based Systems

Efforts to develop descriptions or typologies of offenders based on personality traits has a long history in psychology and criminology (Andrews & Bonta, 2006; Mannheim, 1965; Shoemaker, 1996).

QUAY'S PERSONALITY-BASED SYSTEM

Quay's (1966, 1987) personality-based system is an example of this approach that has proven popular over the years. Table 2.1 defines the five categories within that system, each defining a different type of offender. Youth engaging in chronic serious and violent criminal activity would normally fall within the Aggressive-Psychopathic category.

MILLON ADOLESCENT CLINICAL INVENTORY

A system based on the Millon Adolescent Clinical Inventory (Millon, 1993) is presented as particularly relevant for describing mental disorders in juvenile offenders. The system incorporates a broad range of personality and behavioral dysfunctions potentially relevant to a propensity for antisocial actions. The system includes

Table 2.1 | Five Offender Types in Quay's Classification System

Aggressive-Psychopathic: Aggressive individuals showing little concern about victims; constantly violating rules and searching for excitement.
Manipulative: Similar to Aggressive-Psychopathic group, but uses manipulation and cunning rather than aggressive means.
Situational: Relatively trustworthy offenders with a short criminal history; do not see themselves as criminals and view their conflict with law as transitory.
Inadequate-Dependent: Passive individuals frequently victimized by more aggressive offenders; generally submissive and form immature relationships with others.
Neurotic-Anxious: Usually tense and depressed and do not deal well with stress; also victimized by more aggressive offenders.
Note: From Quay (1966, 1987).

2
chapter

personality patterns, expressed concerns, and clinical syndromes. Table 2.2 identifies the scales within the personality patterns and clinical syndromes domains.

CALLOUS AND UNEMOTIONAL TRAITS

An important line of research endeavoring to identify personality characteristics of youth engaging in violent criminal activity focuses on the concept of *callous and unemotional traits* (Boxer & Frick, 2008; Essau, Sasagawa, & Frick, 2006; Frick, 2006). Youth exhibiting these traits show a general lack of empathy or capacity to experience guilt. This syndrome is considered part of a larger syndrome describing youth with neurologically based learning impairments that interfere with normal socialization and result in temperamental vulnerabilities, poor social information processing, and impulsive tendencies. This syndrome, discussed in more detail in chapter 3, characterizes many youth who exhibit conduct disorders from an early age and who are at high risk for engaging in serious violent behaviors during adolescence and adulthood.

Only a minority of youth exhibiting behavioral manifestations of early neurological disorder display the callous/unemotional

Table 2.2 | Personality and Clinical Scales from the Millon System

Domain	Scales
Personality patterns	Introversive
	Inhibited
	Doleful
	Submissive
	Dramatizing
	Egotistic
	Unruly
	Forceful
	Conforming
	Oppositional
Clinical syndromes	Eating dysfunctions
	Substance abuse proneness
	Delinquency predisposition
	Impulsive propensity
	Anxious feelings
	Depressive affect
	Suicidal tendency

Note: From *Millon Adolescent Clinical Inventory*, by T. Millon, 1993, Minneapolis, MN: National Computer Systems.

pattern, but youth who do are at particularly high risk for engaging in violent criminal actions (Kruh, Frick, & Clements, 2005). Further, both research and clinical experience indicate that efforts to treat youth exhibiting the callous/unemotional syndrome are particularly difficult, although not impossible (Boxer & Frick, 2008).

PSYCHOPATHY

The personality construct of *psychopathy* is closely linked to the callous/unemotional syndromes just described. Hare (1998, 2003) developed the concept of psychopathy as part of an analysis of adult personality disorders associated with serious mental disorders and criminal acts. The concept identifies a set of traits and conditions (e.g., pathological lying, lack of remorse, impulsivity, irresponsibility) associated with serious antisocial actions. The concept of psychopathy has, with some modifications, been applied to adolescents (Forth, Kosson, & Hare, 2003). The youth construct has eliminated some of the traits relevant only to adults and modified others to make them more relevant to juveniles. An assessment instrument, Psychopathy Checklist—Youth Version (Forth et al., 2003), has been developed for measuring the construct.

Although some of the traits represented within the psychopathy construct have relevance to the understanding of youth engaging in serious antisocial behaviors, serious questions have been raised about the use of the psychopathy construct and assessment instrument with children and adolescents (Edens, Skeem, Cruise, & Caufmann, 2001; Seagrave & Grisso, 2002). The criticisms generally focus on the fact that youth often exhibit some of the so-called psychopathic traits during the normal development process. However, these represent transitory states and do not really have significance for later development. The concept of developmental limitations is discussed further later in this chapter.

OTHER PERSONALITY-BASED DESCRIPTIVE SYSTEMS

Other personality-based descriptive systems relevant to juvenile offenders have been presented by Archer, Bolinskey, Morton, and Farris (2003) and Jesness (1988). These systems are capable of providing information about personality and emotional functioning, but they are of limited value in predicting violent behavior. The behavior- and risk-based

BEWARE
The psychopathy construct is problematic with youth because of developmental processes.

systems described subsequently have much greater utility for this purpose. However, the systems are relevant to the identification of responsivity factors useful in formulating case management decisions. For example, youth characterized as Aggressive-Psychopathic likely require a different approach than required by those identified as Inadequate-Dependent.

Behavior-Based Systems

A third approach to developing systems for youth at risk for serious violent crime is based on the empirical analyses of behavioral data. These systems describe the individual in terms of behavioral dimensions rather than discrete categories. Most of the systems are empirically derived from data collected with behavioral observation schedules or behavioral rating scales, some of which will be described in following chapters. The systems generally reflect a conduct or antisocial behavior disorder type of approach where criminal activity is just one manifestation of behavioral maladaption. These systems have usually been developed from the empirical analysis of data from behavioral and rating checklist measures (see chapter 4).

Reviews by Hoge (1999a, 2001), Le Blanc (1998), and Sattler and Hoge (2006) reveal that a large number of these systems have been developed over the years. The system represented in Achenbach's (1999; Achenbach & Rescorla, 2001) System of Empirically Based Assessment will serve as an illustration.

ACHENBACH'S SYSTEM OF EMPIRICALLY BASED ASSESSMENT

This system is based on data collected from the Child Behavior Checklist instruments described in chapter 4. Parent, teacher, and self-report forms of this checklist measure are available. Items on the instruments focus on concrete behavioral manifestations of behavioral maladaption (e.g. "gets in many fights"; "unhappy, sad, or depressed"). The respondent indicates whether the item is true of the young person.

Data collected with the various forms of the Child Behavior Checklist have been analyzed to yield distinct dimensions of

Table 2.3 | Child Behavior Checklist Factor Scores (Males, Ages 6–18)

Total behavior problems score
Broad-band Scores
Internalizing
Externalizing
Narrow-band internalizing scores
Anxious/depressed
Withdrawn/depressed
Somatic complaints
Social problems
Thought problems
Attention problems
Narrow-band externalizing scores
Rule-breaking behavior
Aggressive behavior

Source: Adapted from *Manual for the ASEBA School-Age Forms and Profiles,* by T.M. Achenbach and L. A. Rescorla, 2001, Burlington, VT: University of Vermont, Research Center for Children, Youth, and Families.

behavioral maladaption. Table 2.3 identifies the dimensions that emerged from data provided by the teacher and parent versions of the Child Behavior Checklist for youth in the age group of 6–18 years. These dimensions are arranged hierarchically from the total behavior problem score, through the broad-based internalizing and externalizing scores, to narrow-band scores. The latter refer to specific expressions of behavior problems and are organized as internalizing (e.g., anxious/depressed) and externalizing (e.g., aggressive behavior) problems.

This system provides a basis for describing the behavioral problems of youth that has particular relevance for young persons committing criminal acts, including violent criminal actions. A general advantage of all of these behavior-based systems is that they provide information about specific behaviors associated with a propensity for antisocial behavior. As such, they are particularly useful in assessing needs for case planning and management purposes.

Risk-Based Systems

The systems for characterizing juvenile offenders described in the previous sections are based on offense histories or on personality or behavioral characteristics. However, research discussed in chapter 3 will show increasing evidence that a broad range of risk and protective variables are involved in the initiation and maintenance of youthful antisocial activity. Some of these reside within the individual (e.g., temperament, intelligence, attitudes) whereas others relate to circumstantial factors (e.g., relations with parents, peer group associations, community services). It is clear that antisocial youth display wide individual differences among these variables.

It follows that, to be truly meaningful, descriptions of youthful offenders should take into account not only the pattern of their antisocial behaviors or personality traits or behavioral characteristics, but rather the entire range of individual and circumstantial factors known to be associated with criminal activities.

Chapter 3 describes advances made in the identification of risk and protective factors associated with youth crime and chapter 4 presents some recent advances in developing instruments for assessing those factors. It may be noted here that only limited progress has been made in developing descriptive frameworks incorporating these factors.

STATIC SYSTEMS
Reviews by Hoge (1999a, 2001), Hoge and Andrews (1996); Le Blanc (1998) and Wiebush, Baird, Krisberg, and Onek (1995) reveal that early efforts to develop a risk-based system for describing

Risk Item	Score
1. Severity of Current Offense	_____
Murder, rape, kidnap, escape.. 10	
Other violent 5	
All other 0	
2. Severity of Prior Adjudications	_____
Violent offense 5	
Property offense.. 3	
Other/none... 0	
3. Number of Prior Adjudications	_____
Two or more.. 5	
Less than 2.. 0	
Total items 1–3	_____

Total items 1–3. If score is 10 or higher, score as *secure placement.* If less than 10, score remaining stability items.

4. Age at First Referral	_____
12–13 years of age 2	
14+ 0	
5. History of Mental Health Outpatient Care	_____
• Yes 1	
• No 0	
6. Youth Lived Alone or With Friends at Time of Current Adjudication	_____
• Yes 1	
• No 0	
7. Prior Out-of-Home Placements	_____
• Yes 1	
• No 0	
Total items 1–7	_____

Apply score to the following placement scale:

   10+   Consider for secure
   5–9   Short-Term Placement
   0–4   Immediate Community placement

Figure 2.1   Example of a Static Risk Assessment Instrument

youthful offenders involved the establishment of an overall risk score based on a set of *static risk factors* (e.g., age at first arrest, number of convictions). Figure 2.1 provides an example of a type of risk assessment instrument based largely on static factors. This type of measure has often been used for disposition and placement decisions. However, these static systems have proven unsatisfactory for the same reasons discussed above in connection with offense-based systems. That is, they cover only a limited range of the risk and need factors associated with a propensity for violent offending.

RECENT RISK-BASED SYSTEMS

More recent efforts to develop risk-based systems are empirically derived and based on a wider range of individual and circumstantial factors. These are designed to reflect the most recent research on factors associated with youth crime. The systems incorporate both static and historical risk factors such as age at first arrest and risk factors that can be altered to reduce risk levels. The latter includes variables such as antisocial attitudes and parental supervision practices.

This type of system is represented in research conducted in connection with the Youth Level of Service/Case Management Inventory (Hoge, 2005; Hoge & Andrews, 2002). This system allows the client to be described in terms of an overall risk score based on an evaluation of risks and needs within seven specific areas: offense history, family dynamics, educational achievement/adjustment, peer associations, substance abuse, personality/behavioral adjustment, and attitudes/orientation. The advantage of this approach is that it encourages a comprehensive risk and need profile of the individual. This and similar systems will be described in more detail in chapter 4.

Challenges in Describing the Juvenile Offender

Efforts to describe juvenile offenders have proven useful in developing predictions of the likelihood that the youth will engage in future criminal activity and in guiding decisions about the best approaches for treating the propensity for criminal activity. Those working with youth should be familiar with these systems to enhance understanding of the young person with whom they are working.

However, limitations of the systems should also be recognized. First, as will be discussed in chapter 3, the socialization process is complicated, and gaps exist in understanding the forces at work in that process. Second, and related, children and adolescents are going through a process of developmental change. This means that personality or behavior traits exhibited at one point in time may not reflect those that will emerge in the future. A sensitivity to the developmental process is essential in working with these youth.

BEST PRACTICE

Be sensitive to the developmental process when evaluating youth.

The emerging fields of developmental psychopathology and developmental criminology have significantly advanced our understanding of the developmental process as it impacts mental health (Cicchetti & Cohen, 1995; Cicchetti & Rogosch, 2002; Rutter, Giller, & Hagell, 1998) and antisocial behavior (Farrington, 2004; Grisso & Schwartz, 2000; Guerra, Williams, Tolan, & Modecki, 2008a; Hoge, in press; Thornberry, 2005). Contributions from this literature affecting understanding of the onset, persistence, and desistence from antisocial behavior will be discussed in later chapters, but some cautions emerging from this developmental literature that must be observed in describing youth are of relevance here.

Age, Discontinuity, Comorbidity

Vincent and Grisso (2005) have identified three factors complicating these descriptive efforts. Age relativity refers to the phenomenon that apparently abnormal syndromes appearing at a certain age may in fact reflect normal development at that period. A youth beginning to engage in deception and lying to parents may signify a serious problem or may be part of the adolescent's effort to establish some independence from the adult. The latter is a normal process in the case of most adolescents and does not represent a serious problem condition. Discontinuity in syndromes is another factor affecting the interpretation of youthful behavior. This refers to the phenomenon whereby negative syndromes represent transitory states with little significance for later development. For example, the period of chronic deception may run its course or the youth may "snap out" of his depression. Third, the descriptive efforts can be complicated by comorbidity, the condition where one syndrome may hide other conditions. A substance abuse disorder may also be associated with emotional conditions such as depression or anger, but the latter may go undetected with a narrow focus on the substance abuse disorder.

Cognitive and Psychosocial Immaturity

Cognitive and emotional limitations of the youth may also complicate our efforts to understand the juvenile offender. These capacities evolve over the childhood and adolescent years as a result of neurological developments and life experiences (Dodge, 2003; Dodge & Rabiner, 2004; Rutter et al., 1998). It is important to understand the actual level of functioning of the youth, and the ways in which his capacities differ from that of the mature adult. For example, before cognitive maturity is fully achieved, youth often have difficulty in dealing with abstract constructs or in evaluating alternative points of view. The latter condition is often exhibited through egocentrism and self-absorption, normal conditions in adolescent development. Further, decision-making, self-management, and self-control skills are still developing. The latter is reflected in impaired risk assessment and limited time perspective. Children and adolescents are also limited in the ability to accurately interpret social cues.

Research from the field of developmental neuroscience has also contributed to an understanding of cognitive and psychosocial immaturity in youth (Nelson, 2003). This research demonstrates that the brain structure of youth is less developed than that of adults and that structural features show a clear link between the neurological features and cognitive and psychosocial limitations of adolescents.

Gender and Ethnic Identity

Finally, and as elaborated in later chapters, gender and ethnic identity must be considered in describing and understanding youth engaging in antisocial behavior. Most of the research and much of the clinical attention has focused on male youth from the majority culture. This is changing, but our understanding of female delinquents and antisocial youth from minority cultures is still somewhat limited.

BEWARE
Research is lacking on female delinquents and minority youth.

2
chapter

Empirical Foundations and Limits | 3

T he ability to contribute to legal decisions involving judgments of violence risk and management depends on an understanding of the factors contributing to the commission of violent actions. Although clinical experience is an important guide in forming these judgments, that experience can be enhanced when based on a solid scientific foundation. Fortunately, significant advances in our understanding of youthful antisocial behavior, including acts of violence, are emerging from theory and research in psychology, psychiatry, and criminology. This chapter will provide a discussion of these advances, and information about specific measures and procedures will be presented in chapter 4.

Theoretical efforts to understand the causes of youth violence have a long history, ranging in more modern times from the psychoanalytic perspective of Freud to contemporary integrative theories. These theories have been developed to explain antisocial behaviors in general, but they apply to the analysis of violent actions as well.

Table 3.1 provides an outline of the most important traditional theoretical perspectives on the causes of youth crime. Although these perspectives have largely been supplanted by more modern theories, they remain influential in some respects. For example, the assumptions made in these theories continue to guide policies regarding the treatment of youthful offenders. This is illustrated in systems emphasizing a purely punitive approach to criminal acts based on the assumption of classical theory that violent acts are entirely voluntary, and in systems focusing on ameliorating social conditions reflecting an economic model. More detailed discussions of the traditional theories are provided by Andrews and Bonta (2006) and Shoemaker (1996).

Table 3.1 | Outline of the Traditional Theories of Delinquency

Classical Theories
Criminal behavior is viewed as purposive and willful; individuals engage in criminal activities because they choose to.
Biological Theories
Criminal behaviors including acts of violence are viewed as products of genetically or biologically influenced personality or emotional characteristics.
Psychodynamic Theories
Criminal behavior represents deviant behavior that can be explained by means of psychological processes.
Social Learning Theories
The acquisition of antisocial attitudes and behaviors is explained through learning taking place within social interactions.
Control Theories
Criminal behavior is explained in terms of the individuals' relations with their social environment; failure to develop attachments to social institutions and a lack of commitment to conventional values are the key variables.
Economic/Sociological Theories
This large group of theories locates the causes of criminal behavior in a social, economic, or cultural context; Marxist, anomie, and labeling theories are examples.

Paradigm Shifts in Theoretical and Empirical Analyses of Youth Crime

Compas, Hinden, and Gerhardt (1995) identified three emerging themes in research and theory relating to adolescent development. These involve (a) the formulation of broad integrative ecological models, (b) the discovery of developmental pathways linking childhood, adolescent, and adult behaviors, and (c) the identification of risk and protective factors associated with normal

INFO

Emerging themes in theory and research on juvenile offending are

- broad integrative ecological models
- developmental pathways linking childhood, adolescent, and adult behaviors
- risk and protective factors associated with normal and maladjusted development
- factors associated with desistance from continued antisocial behavior

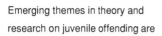

and maladjusted development. These themes have been detected in the analysis of general development, but they are also particularly relevant for the development of a propensity for serious and violent delinquency.

Guerra, Williams, Tolan, and Modecki (2008a) have identified one other important theme in theory and research on juvenile offending. This involves a shift from focusing solely on the predictors of the onset of offending to a concern as well with factors associated with desistance from continued antisocial behavior. Theoretical and empirical developments emerging from these themes have important implications for risk assessment and risk management efforts, as we will see.

3
chapter

Integrative Ecological Models

The fundamental challenge in the search for the causes of antisocial behaviors arises from the complexity of human behavior. Many of the early theoretical positions regarding the causes of criminality focused on a single causal variable, whether poverty, weak ego, deficient self-control, or the XXY chromosome anomaly. These approaches were clearly inadequate. We now know that a wide range of factors can influence the commission of a criminal act. Some of these are internal (e.g., aspects of temperament, social competencies, modes of perception) and some external (e.g., influences of parents and peers, features of the immediate situation in which the action occurs). Further, these factors do not operate in isolation; rather, it is the complex interactions among factors that have causal impact. Further, the dynamics of these factors are complicated. For example, individual predispositions relating to impulsivity and aggressiveness are likely the product of complex interactions among genetic, biological, and environmental influences. Most of the newer theoretical developments attempt to incorporate a broad range of variables that reflect forces operating at the level of the individual, her immediate social environment, and more distal factors within the larger social environment. As such, these theories reflect the broad ecological model of human development advocated by Bronfenbrenner (1979, 1986), Lerner (1991, 1995), and others.

A related development concerns an increased attention to interactions among variables and a concern for the transactional nature of developmental processes. The latter is illustrated in the formulations of the Oregon research group (Patterson, 1982; Patterson, DeBaryshe, & Ramsey, 1989; Patterson, Reid, & Dishion, 1992) in which some forms of antisocial behavior are explained in terms of a coercive reciprocal interaction between parent and child. Antisocial behavior of the youth contributes to dysfunctional parenting, which in turn leads to a further deterioration in child and parent behavior.

A wide range of theories have been advanced to explain the commission of serious antisocial acts, including those of a violent nature. The most satisfactory of the contemporary theories are the developmental life-course theories incorporating a social learning theory perspective into a broad-based integrative framework (see Andrews & Bonta, 2006; Boxer & Frick, 2008; Catalano & Hawkins, 1996; Farrington, 2003, 2004; Frick, 2006; Guerra et al., 2008a; Jessor, 1992; Rutter, 2003; Tolan, Guerra, & Kendall, 1995). An example of a broad-based integrative model is presented next.

Social Development Model

The Catalano and Hawkins' (1996) Social Development Model illustrates the various advances described above: it attempts to integrate a wide range of interacting variables, employs a developmental focus, and incorporates both risk and protective factors. The model is applicable to a range of antisocial behaviors, including violence and substance abuse. Unlike many other theoretical efforts, it also attempts to account for both prosocial and antisocial developmental trajectories.

The authors of the model recognize the importance of adopting a developmental perspective in understanding the way in which antisocial behaviors are acquired. The model also postulates that different processes may be involved in the onset, maintenance, and desistance of the antisocial behaviors, and, further, that the dynamics may differ as a function of the pattern of antisocial behaviors. The factors contributing to occasional and minor offending may be different than those contributing to serious and violent crime.

The Social Development Model describes two paths: one a trajectory leading to a belief in the moral order and a generally prosocial life style and the other a path leading to a belief in antisocial values and a corresponding propensity to antisocial behaviors. The beliefs and values regarding prosocial and antisocial behaviors constitute the most proximal determinants of prosocial and antisocial behaviors. These in turn are a product of four processes:

1. the individual's opportunities for engaging in pro- or antisocial activities;
2. their actual involvement in those activities;
3. their past experience of rewards and punishments for those activities; and
4. their degree of attachment to pro- or antisocial individuals and institutions.

These explanatory concepts are similar to those found in other social control type theories. The Social Development Model departs from those models by postulating a role for individual constitutional factors. These are directly linked to the kinds of skills or competencies the youth exhibits in social situations. To illustrate, the youth may be attached to positive role models at home and in the school but may not have the competencies to function well in these positive environments. This, in turn, may affect the kinds of rewarding experiences he is exposed to. The inclusion of constitutional factors in the model is important because many of the risk and protective factors that have emerged as important from research reflect individual difference variables.

There are a number of strengths associated with this model. First, it represents an effort to incorporate the three paradigm shifts discussed earlier: it integrates a broad range of individual and environmental factors, stresses the importance of identifying developmental pathways, and focuses on risk and protective factors associated with normal and maladjusted development. Second, the model acknowledges that different factors may be associated with the onset, persistence, and desistance from antisocial behaviors.

Explanatory Constructs

The theoretical efforts described above are important in generating and testing hypotheses about the factors influencing the onset and desistance from antisocial behaviors. As such, they are relevant to the following discussions of developmental pathways and the identification of risk factors. However, uncovering explanations for the variables identified in the models and links among the variables often requires another level of theoretical and empirical analysis.

Two examples will be used to illustrate the point. Personality traits related to impulsivity, deficits in attention, and sensation seeking are directly linked in the above models with a propensity for serious and violent criminal activity. However, the source of those traits requires theoretical constructs involving genetic, biological, and environmental considerations. As illustration, Moffitt (2003, 2006) has hypothesized that the dysfunctional personality and behavioral traits are caused at least in part by genetically determined neurological deficits.

A second example is based on hypotheses that parenting practices are directly associated with a propensity for violence. A specific hypothesis supported by research is that harsh punishment links with expressions of physical violence. However, we can raise a question about the mechanisms involved in this punishment–violence link. Explanations for the link involve social learning, heredity, and emotional attachment constructs (Gottfredson & Hirschi, 1990; Widom, 1994).

INFO

Most models of antisocial behavior are dependent on explanatory constructs for theoretical and empirical support.

Research exploring genetic and biological influences on criminal behavior deserves special mention. It is now clear that genetic-based and non-genetic-based biological and neurological factors are linked in some complex ways to a propensity for violence (see Andrews & Bonta, 2006; Rhee & Waldman, 2002). Some investigators (e.g., Caspi et al., 2002) have demonstrated that a variant of a gene involved in neurotransmitter functioning is associated with an elevated risk of violent actions. Importantly, however, they also demonstrated that family environment mediates the link. Youth with this genotype raised in a positive and supportive environment show lower levels of aggressive behavior than those sharing the genotype but raised in a dysfunctional, abusive family environment.

Developmental Pathways

Theoretical analyses of child development have always been concerned with tracking the course of development over the life span. However, as Compas et al. (1995) note, these efforts have usually involved a search for a universal plan that describes all individuals. More recent efforts, though, are based on the assumption that different individuals may traverse different pathways in moving through the developmental sequence and that different forces may affect development at different points in the life span. This seems to be particularly true for antisocial behaviors, with some theorists hypothesizing several different trajectories leading to adolescent and adult criminal activity.

Research in developmental criminology has identified a number of relatively stable patterns or trajectories of antisocial behavior (see Arseneault, Tremblay, Boulerice, & Saucier, 2002; Frick, 2006; Loeber, 1988; Moffitt, 2003, 2006; Reisig, Holtfreter, & Morash, 2006). These patterns describe groups of individuals following similar paths in the expression of criminal behaviors.

Life-Course-Persistent Pattern

One of the paths is particularly relevant to our discussion of serious and violent juvenile offending. The *life-course-persistent* pattern is characterized by youth who exhibit symptoms of a difficult temperament during the early years, the appearance of various forms of conduct and oppositional disorders during the preschool years, an escalation of the incidence and severity of antisocial actions during early childhood and adolescence, and the persistence of the antisocial behaviors into adulthood. These are individuals with a long history of behavioral problems, and they constitute the majority of those we refer to as chronic serious offenders. Their antisocial behaviors may be expressed in nonviolent criminal actions, but many of the youth we encounter who have committed serious violent acts fall within this group.

Adolescent-Limited Trajectory Pattern

The other major pattern identified in the research cited above is referred to as the *adolescent-limited trajectory*. This is characterized by normal development during the childhood years and the more-or-less sudden appearance of antisocial behaviors during adolescence. These youth normally do not engage in serious violent actions, and they usually desist from further criminal actions during later adolescence and the adult years. These are youth who suddenly get into trouble during their teens but revert to a prosocial lifestyle later on. The aggressive actions of these individuals are usually of a proactive nature. Youth exhibiting this pattern are of concern, but they present a somewhat lesser challenge than those who exhibit the life-course-persistent pattern.

Other Patterns and Qualifications

The two patterns discussed above do not characterize all youth who engage in criminal activities. Some do not begin serious criminal activities until adolescence but continue them into adulthood. Another pattern we sometimes observe involves persistent and chronic nonserious criminal activities. These are people who never engage in serious criminal acts but who seem to have continual conflicts with the judicial system.

Although there is considerable support for these developmental patterns, several qualifications should be kept in mind. First, the patterns do not describe all individuals who engage in criminal activities. Second, and related, the evidence clearly shows that the majority of individuals who engage in antisocial activities during childhood and adolescence, whatever the pattern, desist from those actions in adulthood (Nagin & Tremblay, 1999; Sampson & Laub, 2005). Importantly, this means that the majority of youth exhibiting a life-course-persistent pattern during childhood will not continue their criminal activities into adolescence and the adult years.

A third qualification reflects Guerra et al.'s (2008a) point that an analysis of these trajectories must recognize that the course of development is affected not only by characteristics of the individual but also by the contexts in which development takes place. For example, a youth with the behavioral and personality characteristics associated with a propensity for violence may be diverted from that course by an encounter with a strong positive influence.

The Search for Risk and Protective Factors

Identifying individual and situational factors associated with serious criminal acts is important from the point of view of assessing the likelihood that the youth will engage in these actions and for identifying factors that can be modified to reduce the likelihood of engaging in these actions. The terms used in this discussion—risk, needs, responsivity, and protective—were defined in chapter 1.

Risks and Needs Factors

A large number of reviews (Farrington, 1998, 2004, 2006; Hawkins et al., 1998; Heilbrun et al., 2005; Hoge, 2001; Loeber & Farrington, 1998, 2000; Rutter et al. 1998) reveal that considerable advances have been made in identifying risk factors associated with general indices of reoffending in juveniles. Somewhat less information is available regarding factors specifically associated with violent offending, but the reviews above indicate that significant advances are being made here as well.

Table 3.2 identifies the major categories of risk factors associated with serious and violent criminal activity. It is the presence of these factors that contributes to the likelihood that the youth will engage in serious antisocial acts or develop a pattern of criminal activity. Research also supports the view that the accumulation of

Table 3.2 | Major Categories of Risk and Need Factors

Proximal Factors
Prior pattern of conduct disorders/criminal actions
Dysfunctional parenting
Poor school/vocational achievement
Antisocial peer associations
Substance abuse
Poor use of leisure time
Dysfunctional behavior and personality traits
Antisocial attitudes, values, and beliefs
Distal Factors
Criminal/psychiatric problems in family of origin
Family financial problems
Poor accommodations
Negative neighborhood environments

risk factors or the total number of factors constitutes the single best predictor of future criminal activity.

Two types of risk factors are represented in Table 3.2. *Static factors* include those relating to the history of conduct disorder and criminal activity (e.g., age at first arrest, number of convictions); these features of the individual, although relevant for the prediction of future behavior, have no relevance to treatment. *Dynamic or need factors*, on the other hand, are amenable to change. The factors identified in the table are also divided into *proximal factors* that have a direct impact on the criminal action and *distal factors* that operate through the proximal factors. For example, the level of criminality in the neighborhood would affect a youth's risk for engaging in criminality through the influence of parental and peer group attitudes and behaviors.

Although all of the individual and circumstantial factors identified in Table 3.2 are potentially relevant to a propensity for serious and violent criminal activity, the following five categories deserve special attention.

HISTORY OF AGGRESSIVE CONDUCT

Research demonstrates that a history of antisocial behaviors is a significant predictor of both general and violent criminal activity (Farrington, 2004; Heilbrun et al., 2005; Lipsey & Derzon, 1998; Loeber & Farrington 1998, 2000). An early onset of conduct disorders and escalating acts of aggression during childhood consti-

INFO

Relevant risk factors for juvenile violence are

- history of aggressive conduct
- dysfunctional family dynamics/parenting
- antisocial peer group associations
- dysfunctional behavior and personality traits
- antisocial attitudes, values, and beliefs

3
chapter

tutes a major risk factor for violence during adolescence and adulthood. This result emerges clearly from research on life-course-persistent delinquency showing that a high percentage of individuals who engaged in violent actions during adulthood exhibited early levels of aggressive conduct disorders.

This result is somewhat puzzling. Most youth are exposed to negative consequences for aggressive acts, and, in fact, the trend for most is a decline in aggressive acts through adolescence. There are two possible explanations for those cases where the violence persists. Either the youth has experienced a favorable reward/cost value for engaging in aggressive acts or she suffers from a learning impairment that interferes with the learning process (Guerra et al., 2008a; Moffitt, 2003, 2006).

The use of a history of antisocial behavior to evaluate risk is qualified by the finding that many youth exhibiting early conduct disorders desist from antisocial behaviors in adolescence and adulthood. If we were to depend only on criminal history to evaluate risk, we would obtain a very large number of false positives. A history of violent antisocial behavior is also of limited value in developing intervention or rehabilitative strategies because it represents a static factor. Nevertheless, this historical variable does constitute a significant predictor of serious delinquency and needs to be included in the risk assessment.

DYSFUNCTIONAL FAMILY DYNAMICS/PARENTING

There is no question that parents or guardians play a critical role in the emotional and social development of the youth. The biological parent provides the individual's genotype and biological vulnerabilities. For example, early manifestations of difficult temperament are possibly genetically linked, and a mother's use of alcohol or drugs during pregnancy may be associated with neurological deficits. In turn, temperament and neurological deficits can be linked with a propensity for violence (Guerra et al., 2008a; Moffitt, 2003, 2006; Morgan & Lilienfeld, 2000).

Structural and circumstantial features of the family may also be associated with development. These may include absence of a parent, size of the family, mental illness of a parent, living accommodations, or financial status. These factors may directly impact the socialization experience, but more often they function as distal variables affecting the parent's direct treatment of the youth.

The major impact on the youth's development, including the development of a propensity for violence, arises from the emotional relationship between parent and youth and socialization practices. Table 3.3 identifies some constructs representing dysfunctional parenting identified in research as linked with serious and violent delinquency.

The influence of the parent on development is generally highest during the early and middle childhood years, with direct influence declining through adolescence. It is during the early years that the bonding process occurs. Where this process occurs normally, the youth is likely to develop positive and prosocial behaviors, personality traits, and attitudes. Where the emotional bonding process does not proceed normally for whatever reason, the social learning process might be impaired and dysfunctional emotional and social development may occur. There is evidence that the most severe forms of criminal propensity reflected in a callous and unemotional

Table 3.3 | Examples of Dysfunctional Parenting Constructs Linked with Delinquency

Poor supervision
Inappropriate disciplinary techniques
Inconsistent parenting
Poor communication with youth
Poor parent–youth relationship
Emotional abuse
Physical/sexual abuse

orientation occur where normal parent–child bonding is not present (Boxer & Frick, 2008; Frick, 2006).

Although the direct influence of the family and parent declines somewhat during adolescence, the early socialization experience continues an indirect influence through the emotional and social patterns established through that experience. The parent's success at monitoring and influencing the youth's behavior during adolescence is also an important determinant of participation in or desistance from criminal activities.

Any attempt to explain the link between parenting style and the development of the youth must also acknowledge the reciprocal nature of the parent–child relationship (Patterson, 1982). The parent's treatment of the youth is affected by his behavior. On the other hand, the parent's feelings for the youth and treatment are, in turn, affected by the youth's behavior. This is a particular issue with individuals reflecting a life-course-persistent pattern. These youth often exhibit a difficult temperament and tendency toward conduct disorder from an early age. This means they are often difficult to handle, particularly by parents with limited knowledge of effective child-rearing practices or experiencing significant life stress.

Although little control may be exercised over structural aspects of the family, risk factors associated with parenting are amenable to change and can be considered dynamic risk or need factors. For example, effective supervision of the youth's behavior can reduce the risk of delinquency, and this can be modified through parent training programs.

ANTISOCIAL PEER ASSOCIATIONS

Associations with antisocial peers is a significant predictor of both general and serious delinquency. In fact, it can be considered one of the most potent risk factors in the case of adolescents, playing a particular role in adolescent-limited delinquency. However, the form taken by the association and the dynamics of the bond vary. In some cases an early propensity for violence leads the youth to seek out other young people with similar propensities or who at any rate are supportive of antisocial behaviors. In other cases the youth may show little inclination toward violence but will be led toward those actions through the associations. The latter is sometimes observed where a young person is required to engage in some form of serious delinquency as a condition of gang membership. Some evidence exists that the influence of negative peer associations may be even stronger for girls than for boys (Pepler et al., 2005).

Antisocial peer associations is an important risk factor, but this is a problem that can be addressed and should therefore be considered a dynamic risk or need factor. It will not be simple to separate the girl from the antisocial boyfriend or entice the youth from the gang, but there are actions we can take that, where successful, will significantly reduce the level of risk.

DYSFUNCTIONAL BEHAVIORAL AND PERSONALITY FACTORS

The reviews cited above document that certain personality and behavioral traits are closely linked with serious and violent offending. Youth engaging in serious and chronic crime often exhibit signs of impaired learning ability, poor self-control expressed in impulsivity, a propensity for risk taking, and high levels of aggressive emotions. Table 3.4 illustrates the range of behavioral and personality factors identified in this research.

Table 3.4 | Examples of Dysfunctional Personality, Cognitive, and Behavior Traits Linked with Delinquency

Attention/concentration problems
Impulsivity
Poor frustration tolerance
Sensation seeking/high daring
Inflated self-esteem
Low verbal/nonverbal IQ
High aggressive drive
Callous/unemotional

These traits are common among all youth who engage in criminal actions, but they are particularly pronounced in those exhibiting a life-course-persistent pattern involving violent actions. These youth exhibit, often from an early age, high levels of impulsivity, sensation seeking, and callousness. The hypothesis has been advanced that these traits are associated with a more general impairment in learning ability (Guerra et al., 2008a; Moffitt, 2003, 2006; Morgan & Lilienfeld, 2000). This impairment may relate to neurological deficits that interfere with learning. The impairment means that the individual is incapable of acquiring positive modes of responding as the socialization process proceeds.

The concept of a callous and unemotional personality trait was discussed in chapter 2. This identifies youth showing a general lack of empathy or capacity to experience guilt (Boxer & Frick, 2008; Essau et al., 2006; Frick, 2006). Evidence has been presented showing that this trait is linked with violent criminal actions (Kruh, Frick, & Clements, 2005).

Establishing a link between the broader construct of mental disorder and propensity for violence is somewhat problematic (Grisso, 2004; Vincent & Grisso, 2005). As discussed previously, the conduct, disruptive behavior, and substance abuse disorders are

BEWARE
The broader
construct of
mental disorder cannot be
clearly linked to propensity
for violence.

clearly implicated as risk factors. Other disorders such as depression and anxiety are less clearly linked directly with violent behavior. However, two points should be kept in mind in this regard. Many youth involved in antisocial behavior do exhibit these conditions; they are comorbid with antisocial behavior. Second, these may be important responsivity factors to be taken into account in case management planning.

Whatever the source of these dysfunctional behavioral and personality traits, they do represent significant risk factors for the onset and persistence of serious antisocial activities. However, these patterns of behavior and personality can also be considered need factors because they can be altered, and if changed, can reduce the level of risk. Addressing problems such as impulsivity and anger management is not easy, particularly in the case of violent youth, but techniques of management do exist (see Boxer & Frick, 2008; Guerra et al., 2008b; Tate, Reppucci, & Mulvey, 1995).

ANTISOCIAL ATTITUDES, VALUES, AND BELIEFS

Research on the correlates and causes of serious and violent crime has also shown that attitudes and beliefs held by the youth are closely associated with antisocial behaviors, including violent actions. These may be reflected in negative feelings about parents, teachers, police, judges, teachers, or others in positions of authority. One important characteristic of youth with a propensity for violence is a detachment or alienation from symbols of authority. This alienation may be associated with negative experience with authorities, but more often the association is with a more general alienation established earlier in the socialization process. The following items from the *How I Think Questionnaire (HITQ;* Gibbs, Barriga, & Potter, 2001), a self-report measure of antisocial attitudes and reasoning, illustrate this type of attitude:

- Everybody breaks the law, it's no big deal.
- If I really want to do something, I don't care if it's legal or not.
- Stores make enough money that it's OK to take things you need.

The early theory and research of Kohlberg (1984) suggested that the moral reasoning processes of adolescents explain in part their engagement in antisocial activities. This work has been considerably extended through more recent empirical work on the moral reasoning and social perception processes of children and adolescents.

INFO

Developmental limitations may exacerbate antisocial behavior in youth.

The research of Cauffman and Steinberg (2000) and Scott, Reppucci, and Woolard (1995) has shown that certain aspects of moral reasoning develop gradually over the adolescent years and that, until full maturity is reached, adolescents may display important limitations in reasoning and decision-making powers. These limitations include a limited capacity for independent decision making, a short- rather than long-term time perspective, a limited ability to experience empathy, and a limited capacity to exercise self-constraint or self-control. All adolescents exhibit these developmental limitations to one degree or another, but where combined with other risk factors, they often lead the youth to serious antisocial actions.

Another line of research focuses on the social perception process (Dodge, 1986; Dodge & Rabiner, 2004). This work has demonstrated that antisocial behaviors, particularly those involving aggression, sometimes derive from biased or impaired processing of social cues. These involve tendencies to interpret neutral or ambiguous social approaches as hostile, to focus on aggressive social cues, and to hold positive beliefs about aggression. This type of thinking is illustrated in the following sample items from the HITQ:

- People need to be roughed up once in a while.
- It's no use trying to stay out of fights.
- People are always trying to hassle me.

Antisocial attitudes, values, and beliefs should be treated as dynamic risk factors. These can be altered through counseling and therapy, and to the extent they are replaced with more positive ways of thinking risk for continued antisocial behavior will be reduced.

3
chapter

OTHER RISK AND NEED FACTORS

Table 3.2 identifies a number of other risk and need factors that may be associated with serious and violent delinquent acts, although in most they play a supplementary rather than direct role in the development of the propensity. For example, school failure and poor use of leisure time are often the consequence of the engagement in antisocial activities. An exception is substance abuse, a factor that can contribute directly to the commission of a serious crime when the act is for obtaining drugs or alcohol or when the substance may reduce inhibitions toward the commission of the act.

Only limited research is available at present for identifying risk factors associated with violent sexual offending on the part of adolescents (see Barbaree & Marshall, 2006; Ryan & Lane, 1997). Many of the risk factors identified above as associated with violent offending may also be exhibited by youth committing sexual offenses. Worling and Langstrom (2006) identify the following as additional potential risk factors:

- A history of sexual offenses
- Deviant sexual interests
- Attitudes supportive of sexual offending
- Sexual preoccupation
- Social isolation

An instrument designed for assessing risk for sexual reoffending is described in chapter 5.

Responsivity Factors

These have been defined as characteristics of the youth or her circumstances that, although not directly related to the criminal activity, should be taken into account in case planning. They are relevant, in other words, to the case management process. To illustrate, a young woman may be engaging in criminal activity in response to conflicts with parents and involvement with an antisocial gang. However, she may also be suffering from a mood disorder such as depression, and this would have to be acknowledged in developing an intervention to deal with the family and peer issues. Intelligence, reading ability, readiness for treatment, and pathological conditions such as depression or anxiety disorder are examples.

The concept of responsivity also encompasses interactions between characteristics of the youth and the intervention. Not all interventions are appropriate for all youth, and it is here that sensitivity to personality and emotional features of the youth becomes important. For example, girls who have experienced serious abuse from a male may not respond as well to a male as opposed to a female counselor.

Protective Factors

Protective factors are defined as those that mediate or buffer the effects of the risk factors. The presence of these factors enables the individual to cope better with adverse circumstances. A positive temperament, interest in sports, and the availability of a supportive adult are examples of resilience factors that can negate or moderate the effects of risk. Table 3.5 identifies a range of protective or strength factors. Note, however, that there continues to be some uncertainty regarding the way in which risk and protective factors interact with one another (Rutter, 2000; Rutter et al., 1998). It is not completely clear, for example, whether the protective factor protects the individual from risk or whether the factor simply ameliorates the effects of risk. Theoretical debates aside, it is important to identify protective or resilience characteristics in the assessment process.

Other Considerations Regarding Risk, Need, Responsivity, and Resilience

Theoretical and empirical efforts have advanced our understanding of responsivity, resilience, and, in particular, risk and need. The relevance of this work for developing practical assessment tools and management strategies will be discussed in later chapters. However, there are a number of points to keep in mind in considering our understanding of these concepts.

GENERALIZING ACROSS GROUPS

Knowledge of the risk and need factors associated with the risk of serious and violent delinquency is extensive and growing. Most of

3
chapter

Table 3.5 | Examples of Protective/Strength Factors

Individual Factors	High self-esteem
	Positive, prosocial attitudes
	Good social skills
	Good problem-solving skills
	Strong academic skills, motivation
	Interest in sport, hobby
	Physical health
Family Factors	Competent parents
	Cooperative parents
	Other supportive family member
	Financial stability
	Small family size
Situational Factors	Good schools
	Good mental health services
	Positive neighborhood
	Recreational facilities
	Positive, supportive peers

the research has been conducted with Caucasian and African American male adolescents in North America. Although the evidence is limited, research suggests that risk factors are similar for Caucasian and African American youth (see Redding & Arrigo, 2005). It is likely that the higher levels of antisocial behavior observed in African American samples are a result of higher levels of many of the risk factors. Research also suggests that risk factors are the same for male and female adolescents (Moffitt, Caspi,

Rutter, & Silva, 2001; Rowe, Vazonyi, & Flannery, 1995; Schwalbe, 2008; Simourd & Andrews, 1994). Although the research that has been reported for other minorities within North American society or for other cultures and societies is not extensive, clinical experience would suggest that the risk and need factors identified in Table 3.2 have considerable generality across cultures.

BEST PRACTICE

When assessing risk and need factors, keep in mind their

- generality across groups
- role in the developmental process
- relationship to onset, persistence, and desistance
- links with the immediate situation

ROLE IN THE DEVELOPMENTAL PROCESS

Previous discussions emphasized that the relative influence of the risk and need factors will vary with developmental level. Family factors will likely be paramount during the earlier childhood years, whereas peer group experiences will emerge as increasingly important through adolescence. Similarly, leisure time activities and substance abuse will increase in influence during the later years. Behavioral, personality, and attitudinal characteristics will be important across the childhood and adolescent years, but these too are subject to change. For example, we normally expect that moral reasoning ability will mature as the youth gets older.

It is important to recognize that the nature and influence of responsivity and protective factors may change with time. For example, mood disorders such as depression become more common during adolescence, and the availability of positive peer models can become an increasingly important protective factor.

The MacArthur Foundation is currently conducting a major longitudinal study of factors associated with desistance from criminal activity during late adolescence and the early adult years. This research, under the direction of Edward Mulvey, should provide important information to guide intervention efforts. The Pathways to Desistance study is an ongoing, longitudinal study of serious juvenile offenders transitioning into adulthood. The study seeks to capture how maturity, life changes, and involvement in the justice system all relate to desistance from crime. Data collection for the study will be completed in 2010.

ONSET, PERSISTENCE, AND DESISTANCE

Guerra et al. (2008a) have called attention to the fact that most research on juvenile delinquency has focused on factors and conditions associated with the onset and persistence of criminal activity. Less attention has been paid to factors associated with desistance. Why, for example, does the 14-year-old youth with a history of increasingly serious antisocial behavior cease those activities and begin showing positive adjustment? Have the risk factors simply disappeared or has the youth been exposed to strength or protective factors to counter the risk? If the latter, what are the critical resilience conditions? Knowledge of the need, responsivity, and resilience factors involved here is limited, but it is important to be sensitive to the issue in developing management strategies.

ROLE OF THE IMMEDIATE SITUATION

Several of the theories cited at the beginning of this chapter, including Andrews and Bonta's (2006) Psychology of Criminal Conduct model, stress the importance of considering the immediate situation in which the crime occurs. Even though a youth's commission of an antisocial act depends on the individual characteristics she brings to the situation, the actual commission of the act depends on perceptions of the circumstances being confronted. Research has as yet provided relatively little guidance on linking individual risk factors with situations (Grisso, 2003; Heilbrun, 1997).

Developing predictions with reference to specific situations arises in the context of targeted or dangerousness assessments. The issue in this case is the likelihood that the youth will engage in an act of violence in a particular situation or directed toward a specific individual (Borum, Fein, Vossekuil, & Bergland, 1999; Fein et al., 2002). These predictions are often used in evaluating threats of violent actions in school or custody settings. These assessments require a range of both clinical and standardized instruments and procedures (Fein et al., 2002).

Implications for Risk and Management Assessments

BEWARE
Watch for gaps in knowledge about the factors affecting antisocial youth.

The review of theory and research in this chapter reveals considerable progress in our understanding of the factors contributing to antisocial behavior of youth, particularly serious and violent criminal activity. The following chapters will indicate the ways in which this knowledge has been translated into practical guidelines for assessing and managing the violent behavior of juveniles. However, a note of caution is needed. Our knowledge in this area has significantly advanced, but gaps in this knowledge still exist, and this must be kept in mind when evaluating the practical guidelines. These issues will be pursued further in the following chapters.

3
chapter

APPLICATION

Preparation for the Evaluation | **4**

T his chapter will provide a discussion of ethical and legal issues relevant to planning the assessment process as well as issues in the selection of appropriate tools and procedures. Chapter 5 reviews practical issues in the conduct of assessments, including a discussion of specific measuring instruments.

It is important to keep in mind the purpose of the violence risk assessment when planning the assessment process. Risk assessments are required in a variety of clinical and legal contexts. Where conducted within legal contexts they generally have a specific purpose, whether assessing risk of violence for detention, transfer, or sentencing purposes. As indicated above, the forensic assessment may also be asked to provide information about managing the risk. In any case, the specific purpose of the assessment must guide the preparation phase.

Ethical and Legal Concerns

Assessments of risk and need factors may guide important forensic decisions about the offender, including pretrial detention, pre- and postcharge diversion, waiver to the mental health system, or dispositions and sentencing. The importance of these decisions places a burden on the system to ensure that relevant legal and ethical guidelines are followed.

The legal system through the federal courts has provided broad guidelines to ensure that due process is followed in the processing of juveniles through the justice system (e.g., *in re Gault*, 1967; *Kent v. United States*, 1966). These guidelines

BEST PRACTICE

Plan for the risk assessment in accordance with its specific purpose.

apply to the treatment of youth at all phases of the process from arrest through disposition. The state juvenile justice systems generally provide statutory guidelines as well.

On the other hand, there are few specific legal guidelines regarding the conduct of risk/need assessments. The exceptions relate to decisions regarding referrals to the adult judicial or mental health systems. In these cases statute or policy may specify the terms of the assessment although even here considerable latitude may exist (Grisso, 1998, 2003).

Although few legal guidelines exist regarding the conduct of risks and needs assessments in juvenile justice system, standards and procedures do exist where these are conducted by mental health professionals.

Standards for Assessment

Professional guidelines for the conduct of assessments have been developed by a number of professional associations, primarily psychological and psychiatric groups. Table 4.1 lists the major sources of assessment guidelines. Some of the guidelines—such as those developed by the Committee on Ethical Guidelines for Forensic Psychologists (1991)—apply specifically to the conduct of assessments in judicial settings and others apply broadly to the conduct of psychological and psychiatric assessments.

The Standards of Educational and Psychological Testing (American Educational Research Association, American Psychological Association, & National Council on Measurement in Education, 1999) constitute a particularly important source of standards for psychological assessments. The Standards provide rigorous guidelines regarding the construction, application, and interpretation of all formal psychological assessments. The major sections of the Standards are outlined in Table 4.2.

Guidelines relating to the conduct of assessments with youth from culturally diverse backgrounds are also available. The American Psychological Association (1990) Guidelines for Providers of Psychological Services to Ethnic, Linguistic, and Culturally Diverse Populations is an example. The DSM-IV-TR also provides guidelines for assessing risk in youth from minority groups.

Table 4.1 | Sources of Guidelines and Standards for Mental Health Assessments

Code of Fair Testing Practices in Education (American Psychological Association, 1988)
Standards for Educational and Psychological Testing (American Educational Research Association, American Psychological Association, & National Council on Measurement in Education, 1999)
Speciality Guidelines for Forensic Psychologists (Committee on Ethical Guidelines for Forensic Psychologists, 1991)
Ethical Guidelines for the Practice of Forensic Psychiatry (American Academy of Psychiatry and the Law, 1995)
Guidelines for Providers of Psychological Services to Ethnic, Linguistic, and Culturally Diverse Populations (American Psychological Association, 1990)
Ethical Principles of Psychologists and Code of Conduct (American Psychologist, 2002)
Guidelines for Computer-Based Tests and Interpretations (American Psychological Association, 1986)

4
chapter

Table 4.2 | Outline of the Standards for Educational and Psychological Testing

Part I: Technical Standards for Test Construction and Evaluation
Standards relating to validity, reliability, test construction, scaling, and normative data are presented. The section also includes guidelines regarding information to be included in manuals and user guides.
Part II: Professional Standards for Test Use
Detailed standards regarding the actual application of assessments. It includes statements about the qualifications of assessors and specific guidelines for the administration and interpretation of assessments. Recommendations regarding the use of assessments within specific settings (e.g., schools, organizations) are also presented.

(Continued)

Table 4.2 | (Continued)

Part III: Standards for Particular Applications
Guidelines regarding the use of assessment tools with linguistic minorities and handicapped individuals are presented in this section.
Part IV: Standards for Administrative Practice
Ethical issues relating to informed consent, confidentiality, labeling, and the sharing of assessment information are considered in this final section of the Standards.

Note. Standards for Educational and Psychological Testing, by American Educational Research Association, American Psychological Association, and National Council on Measurement in Education, 1999, Washington, DC: Author.

Professional Regulation

The establishment of standards and guidelines for assessment is one issue, the enforcement of those standards is another. The application of legal remedies constitutes, of course, one way in which these activities are regulated. Beyond this level, though, regulation becomes somewhat problematic because different professional groups are involved in the conduct of assessments.

Two levels of regulation apply to the psychology and psychiatric professions. The first is through nonregulatory, voluntary bodies. The most important of these are the national groups such as the American, Canadian, and British psychological and psychiatric associations. Smaller groups include the various state associations and specialized groups such as the National Association of School Psychologists and the American Board of Clinical Neuropsychology. All have adopted codes of conduct, including standards regarding assessments. Membership in the organizations is voluntary, but members are obligated to observe their ethical standards.

The second level of regulation occurs through regulatory bodies of professional mental health providers. Membership in these regulatory bodies is mandatory for all psychologists and psychiatrists conducting clinical activities. These are created by acts of

the state legislatures and serve to regulate mental health professionals in the respective jurisdictions. These bodies constitute the
major means for ensuring the ethical conduct of assessments by
psychologists and psychiatrists.

Major Ethical and Legal Concerns

The various guidelines and standards outlined in Table 4.1 present
detailed information concerning ethical issues arising in connection
with the conduct of psychological assessments. The volumes by
Bersoff (1995) and Eyde et al. (1993) also provide useful discussions of these issues. Grisso (1998, 2003), Grisso and Vincent
(2005), and Grisso and Schwartz (2000) have discussed ethical
issues specific to forensic assessments.

DUE PROCESS

A key issue in the conduct of forensic assessments concerns ensuring
that due process rules are followed:

> For youth who are charged with delinquencies, the juvenile justice
> system has a mandate to insure that the legal process judges their
> responsibility for their alleged delinquencies fairly, and that the
> system does not abuse its discretion deciding on penalties and
> rehabilitative measures when youths are found delinquent. (Grisso,
> 2005a, p. 9)

As indicated above, rules governing due process have been established by the federal courts and state jurisdictions. It is the responsibility of the mental health professional to be aware of the laws and
regulations.

ASSESSMENT INSTRUMENTS AND PROCEDURES

An important ethical issue concerns the
appropriateness and fairness of the assessments employed in a particular situation.
As discussed above, it is necessary to ensure
that instruments and procedures have
demonstrable reliability and validity for
the individual being assessed and for the

**BEST
PRACTICE**

Be aware of the laws and
regulations regarding the due
process of youth applicable in
your jurisdiction.

purposes with which they are being used. Further, if scores are to be interpreted with reference to normative samples, the samples must be relevant to the individual being assessed.

INFORMED CONSENT

Informed consent constitutes another important ethical consideration in forensic assessments. Where the assessment is ordered by the court, it is not necessary to obtain informed consent. However, the youth should be fully appraised of the nature and purpose of the assessment and any limits on confidentiality associated with the assessment. The client should also be warned of any consequences associated with a refusal to participate in the process (Melton, Petrila, Poythress, & Slobogin, 2007).

Assessment always constitutes in some sense an invasion of the individual's privacy. Under most circumstances that invasion is justified only where the individual has freely consented to the action. The question of capacity to understand the terms of the assessment becomes somewhat complicated in the case of children and adolescents, but in most cases adolescents are considered capable of this understanding, and obtaining their consent (rather than approaching the parent) is generally considered appropriate.

The informed consent procedures must take care to communicate the uses that are to be made of the assessments, and then efforts must be made to ensure that no other uses are made of the information. This can be a special problem in the case of forensic assessments where information collected in early stages of processing may be used later in the adjudication phase. It is important for the system to have clear rules in place regarding the uses that will be made of the assessment information (Grisso & Vincent, 2005).

Informed consent is required for all other evaluations of the juvenile and for the collection of information from collaterals. The client should be informed about the purpose and procedures of the assessment and of all uses to be made of the information collected. Care must be taken to ensure that the youth fully understands the terms of the assessment. It is important for systems to have in place clear rules regarding the uses of information collected in forensic assessments (Grisso & Vincent, 2005).

IMMEDIATE THREAT OF VIOLENCE

A special issue sometimes arises in the case of forensic violence risk assessments, and this occurs where the professional concludes that the youth poses an immediate threat of physical violence. Under these circumstances the professional is normally responsible for notifying the appropriate authorities immediately. However, caution must be exercised in concluding that an immediate threat exists. Calling this to the attention of authorities is likely to have serious consequences for the youth and harm can arise where the threat does not actually exist.

BEST PRACTICE

Obtain informed consent from youth and collaterals, making clear how the information will be used and the limits of confidentiality.

FOCUS OF RESPONSIBILITY

A more general ethical issue confronting the mental health provider concerns focus of responsibility. In a forensic context, a psychologist evaluating a youth is responsible for providing the best information possible to the legal system to facilitate informed decision making. In some cases the information may be favorable to the youth's situation and in other cases not. The basic responsibility of the assessor in forensic situations is to "call it as she sees it."

Rules applying to forensic assessments are different than those applying to assessments conducted in therapeutic situations (Grisso & Appelbaum, 1998; Grisso & Vincent, 2005). The important point is to ensure that client confidentiality is protected to the extent possible within the legal guidelines governing the assessment. This may mean that under some circumstances information revealed in the assessment will not be reported because it is not relevant to the forensic issue. Again, the client must be fully informed of any limits on confidentiality. The youth may require access to legal representation to ensure that all ethical and due process rules are observed in the assessment. Additional considerations regarding the reporting of risk assessments will be discussed in the following chapters.

4
chapter

Clinical Versus Standardized/Actuarial Assessments

It is customary to distinguish three general approaches to the conduct of forensic assessments. Unstructured clinical assessments are based on a relatively unstructured collection of information and a dependence on subjective judgments of the assessor. Actually, more or less structure may be represented in the information collection, with one extreme defined by a completely idiosyncratic approach and the other by the use of a checklist or schedule to guide information collection. As well, the use of the information to form a judgment can be informed by more or less expertise as contrasted by the prosecutor with little background in assessing mental disorder with a psychiatrist who is able to draw on considerable expertise in his clinical diagnosis.

Clinical Judgment

Many assessments of violence risk in forensic settings reflect a clinical approach and are conducted in informal, unstructured ways by individuals with little background or expertise in evaluating violent behavior in children and adolescents. This includes many of the police, prosecutors, other court personnel, and detention and correctional officers involved in these decisions. Research will be discussed subsequently demonstrating that limited reliability and validity are associated with *clinical judgments*, particularly in comparison to more *standardized assessment* procedures.

Standardized Assessments

Standardized assessments represent structured formats for the collection and synthesis of information. The Wechsler Intelligence Scale for Children—Fourth Edition (WISC-4; Wechsler, 2004) is an example of a standardized assessment. Item content is fixed as are the response options and scoring and interpretation procedures.

Some standardized instruments are also referred to as *actuarial assessments* because they are based on empirically derived items and yield quantitative indices based on normative data. These are also referred to as objective or mechanistic measures because the scores are based on empirically derived equations or actuarial tables. An example is the Level of Service/Case Management Inventory (LS/CMI; Andrews, Bonta, & Wormith, 2004) for assessing adult offenders that yields empirically derived scores reflecting the individual's probability of reoffending over a specified period of time. Two actuarial measures yielding estimates of risk for offending in youth are described below.

Structured Professional Judgments

The third general category of assessments includes guided clinical assessments or *structured professional judgments* (Borum, 2006; Webster, Hucker, & Bloom, 2002). These incorporate structured assessments into the clinical process. The measures are usually in the form of structured checklists or interview guides, with the items empirically derived from data on links with the outcome variable of interest (e.g., violent reoffending). These assessments do not yield quantitative indices of risk but do provide a basis for clinical judgments about risk.

Research: Clinical Versus Standardized Assessments

As indicated, considerable research has been conducted on the relative efficacy of clinical and standardized assessments (Grove & Meehl, 1996; Grove, Zald, Lebow, Snitz, & Nelson, 2000). The research consistently demonstrates that standardized assessments, whether actuarial or structured professional judgments, yield better predictions of future behavior than unstructured clinical assessments. Much of that research has been conducted with adult samples, but because this research is exploring basic assessment processes, there is good reason to believe that the conclusions would also apply to the assessment of risk in youth (Borum, 2006; Hoge, 2008). The superiority of the use of standardized assessments is also supported by the best-practice research discussed earlier: systems employing standardized assessments are more effective than those depending on informal or clinical procedures.

BEST PRACTICE

Use standardized assessment procedures—that is actuarial assessments or structured professional judgment—instead of relying on unstructured clinical judgment.

Screening Versus Assessment

A distinction is sometimes made between screening and assessment procedures, although the line between these is not always entirely clear.

Screening Instruments

Screening instruments are generally relatively simple measures designed for use with all individuals within a group. The Massachusetts Youth Screening Instrument—Version 2 (MAYSI-2; Grisso & Barnum, 2003), for example, is a self-report form used as a preliminary screening device for detecting emotional, behavioral, and psychological disturbances. It does not yield psychological diagnoses but does provide initial information about symptoms that may require more intensive assessments.

Two related advantages of screening tools may be identified. First, these instruments are economical because they can usually be administered and interpreted by non-mental-health professionals. Second, and related, the use of inexpensive screening procedures enables us to assess larger numbers of individuals. This is often a consideration in juvenile justice systems where, because of limited resources, many youth receive little or no assessment.

The major drawback associated with screening procedures relates to the limits on reliability and validity associated with the use of those procedures. The psychometric properties of these measures are usually weaker than those associated with more intensive psychological assessments. The extent to which this represents a drawback depends partly on the actual reliability and validity of the screening devices but also on the uses being made of them.

Assessment Instruments

Assessment instruments, on the other hand, generally involve a more intensive and thorough analysis of psychological or behavioral functioning. This might, for example, involve a comprehensive evaluation of cognitive and personality functioning through the use of standardized tests and clinical interviews. This would be appropriate where signs of serious disorder are present. Many psychological assessments will require the services of a mental health practitioner such as a psychiatrist or a psychologist, but, as will be shown later in this chapter, forensic assessment instruments are available for use by non-mental-health professionals with special training.

Deciding on the Range and Sources of Information

BEST PRACTICE

Collect information from a range of sources, for example

● interviews
● standardized measures
● personality tests
● risk/needs assessment instruments

Research reviewed in chapter 3 indicated that many factors may influence the likelihood a youth will engage in a violent action. These include a prior history of antisocial behaviors, personality and emotional characteristics, attitudes, values, and beliefs, and the current environmental circumstances of the youth. Forming valid judgments about a risk for violence depends on accurate information about these factors.

A range of information sources should be used in collecting the relevant information. Although there may be ethical or legal issues in accessing official files (e.g., probation reports, school assessments, police reports), these can be a useful source of information about characteristics of the youth and her circumstances.

4
chapter

Interviews

An interview with the youth will constitute the major source of information in a violence risk assessment. Although information revealed in the interview must be interpreted with caution, it can yield critical data regarding prior and current behaviors, personality and emotional characteristics, attitudes, and environmental circumstances. Issues in conducting interviews will be explored in more detail in chapter 5.

Interviews with collaterals can also be an important source of relevant information. This includes parents, teachers, and professionals (e.g., police, probation officers) with earlier contact with the youth. Evaluating conflicting information from interviews and files sometimes presents special challenges and resolving those conflicts generally depends on the judgments of the assessor.

Standardized Measures

Both mental health professionals and non-mental-health providers such as probation officers and youth workers may also be able to use some of the standardized rating scales and checklist measures described in chapter 5 to supplement interview information about behavioral, emotional, and attitudinal characteristics of the youth. These may be self-report measures completed by the youth or instruments completed by parents, teachers, or other respondents. For example, the Child Behavior Checklist (CBCL; Achenbach & Rescorla, 2001) is a standardized checklist measure of behavioral pathologies completed by parents or teachers that can be interpreted by probation officers with some training.

Personality Tests

Full psychological assessments conducted by a psychologist or psychiatrist may also involve administration of standardized personality tests. They may also utilize standardized aptitude or achievement measures to evaluate cognitive competencies, although a consideration of those measures lies outside the scope of this review.

Risk/Needs Assessment Instruments

A final and important category of measures includes the broad-based risk/needs assessment instruments, examples of which will be presented in chapter 5. These are generally in the form of structured interview schedules or checklists and involve either an actuarial or a structured professional judgment approach. They are designed for assisting in the collection and synthesis of information relevant to assessing the likelihood of either general or violent criminal actions. Some of these instruments are appropriate for use by only certified mental health professionals, and others may also be used by non-mental-health professionals such as probation officers with special training in use of the instruments.

Psychometri Considerations

Selection of a standardized assessment instrument or procedure should be based on a review of its psychometric properties, with

Table 4.3 | Basic Psychometric Terms

Reliability
The stability or consistency of a measure; formally defined as the relative proportion of true or error variance within a measure.
Content Validity
The adequacy with which a measure represents the conceptual domain it is expected to encompass.
Construct Validity
The theoretical meaning of scores from a measure; the accuracy with which the measure represents the construct in question.
Criterion-Related Validity
Extent to which scores from a measure relate to a criterion of performance; the two forms of criterion-related validity are concurrent and predictive validity.
Dynamic Predictive Validity
The sensitivity of a measure to changes in the dimension being assessed; also referred to as treatment validity.
Incremental Predictive Validity
The extent to which a measure exhibits improvements in prediction relative to other procedures.

4
chapter

particular attention to reliability and validity. Definitions of these constructs are presented in Table 4.3, and Grisso (2005b), Hoge (2008), and Hoge and Andrews (1996) have provided discussions of the constructs as applied to forensic assessments.

BEST PRACTICE

Select a standardized assessment instrument or procedure based on a review of its psychometric properties, with particular attention to reliability and validity.

Reliability

Reliability refers to the stability or consistency of a measure. More formally, it refers to the relative proportion of true and error variance in a measure. Three standard procedures are available for evaluating reliability: *test–retest*, *inter-rater agreement*, and *internal consistency*. Each provides a somewhat different approach to detecting the extent to which extraneous or error factors affect scores on a measure. Reliability coefficients are generally expressed through correlation coefficients.

Reliability constitutes an essential condition in a measure. Lack of stability or consistency in a measure seriously interferes with its utility in applied assessment situations. If, for example, we found that scores on a personality test were affected by factors not related to the personality trait being assessed and that scores fluctuated in a more-or-less random fashion over time, we would have little confidence in that measure.

Validity

Validity is a more difficult construct to define because it is used in a number of different ways in different contexts. However, where referring to psychological tests or procedures, the term refers in its broadest sense to the meaningfulness of scores from a measure (Messick, 1995). Table 4.3 defines a number of different forms of validity, but only two will be noted in our discussion.

CONSTRUCT VALIDITY

Construct validity is sometimes regarded as the key form of validity and may be defined as referring to the theoretical meaning or accuracy of a measure. It is also often defined as referring to the extent to which a measure is measuring what it says it is measuring.

Some illustrations of the definition may be useful. In raising a question of the construct validity of an intelligence test we would be raising a question about the meaningfulness of scores from the test. Just what does a full-scale score of 113 mean so far as the cognitive functioning of the youth is concerned? We could also ask how well that score reflects what we consider the meaning of "intelligence." Consider a second example. If we raised a question about the construct validity of a measure of behavioral pathology we would be asking about the actual meaning of scores from the measure. How do those scores define behavioral pathology? Construct validity may be evaluated through theoretical and empirical procedures.

CRITERION-RELATED

Criterion-related validity is a second form of validity important for our purposes. It refers to the extent to which scores on a measure relate to some criterion of performance. The two forms of criterion-related validity are *concurrent validity* (where predictor and criterion scores are collected at the same time) and *predictive validity* (where predictor scores are collected at one point and criterion scores at a later time).

Criterion-related predictive validity is particularly important in risk assessments because we are concerned with the ability of the assessment score to predict later antisocial actions, specifically violent actions in the present case. This issue is discussed in chapter 5.

4
chapter

Normative Scores

One additional psychometric construct needs to be noted. *Normative scores* reflect performance on a measure relative to the performance of a group of respondents. For example, the YLS/CMI yields information indicating where a total risk score from an individual stands relative to a sample of juvenile offenders.

However, the value of scores expressed relative to a normative sample depends on the extent to which that sample adequately reflects the population represented by the individual being assessed. It would make little sense to evaluate an individual risk score from a 12-year-old male relative to the risk score of a 17-year-old.

Practical Considerations

The following is a discussion of practical issues in the selection of instruments or procedures for the forensic assessment.

Relevance to the Purpose of the Assessment

A choice of assessment measure or procedure should be guided, first, by the purposes of the assessment. There would be little value, for example, in using a personality test to aid in a decision about pretrial detention or an intelligence test to guide a decision about length of probation. Ethical and sometimes legal considerations dictate that a psychological assessment must be appropriate to the decision in question.

Forensic decisions are often narrow in scope, requiring, for example, a judgment about competence to waive *Miranda* rights or competence to stand trial. In some cases specialized forensic measures such as the MacArthur Competence Assessment Tool—Criminal Adjudication (MacCAT-CA; Poythress et al., 1999) might be available.

However, decisions requiring judgments of a youth's propensity for committing a violent act often raise more difficult assessment issues. The broad-based risk/need assessment instruments discussed earlier in the chapter generally yield either actuarial or structured judgments of risk for general reoffending, although in most cases research is offered to support their predictive validity with violent offending as well. However, care must be taken in interpreting the risk estimates yielded by these measures because of limits on their predictive validity and because they tend to focus broadly on violent offending rather than specific forms of violence in specific situations. This issue will be explored more fully in chapter 5.

The selection of assessment tools is somewhat easier where the concern is with assessing need factors for case management decisions (Heilbrun, 1997). As indicated in chapter 3, knowledge of the risk and need factors associated with violent behavior is well advanced. Further, as shown above, a wide range of well-researched assessment tools are available. For example, it is clear that certain antisocial attitudes and beliefs are closely associated with violent actions. As indicated earlier in the chapter, a number of validated attitude measures are available for assessing these factors.

Relevance to the Individual Assessed

It is important to ensure that the assessment instrument is appropriate for the individual being assessed. This depends in part on the availability of normative scores appropriate to the youth as well as reliability and validity data supporting use of the measure for the group from which the youth is drawn. For example, a personality test developed and evaluated with samples of boys between 8 and 12 years may not be relevant for a 17-year-old girl. Age, gender, ethnic group membership, and the presence of physical or mental handicaps are among the factors that should be considered in selecting assessment tools. Many of the standardized aptitude, personality, and behavioral measures have been evaluated

BEST PRACTICE

Consider factors relevant to the individual when choosing an assessment tool, including the youth's

● age,

● gender,

● ethnic group membership, and

● physical or mental handicaps.

for a wide range of respondent types, but this is not true of all instruments, and it is important to keep this issue in mind in selecting assessment tools. The issue of cultural and ethnic considerations will be considered further in chapter 5.

Dealing With Cultural and Ethnic Differences

The juvenile justice system must often deal with native-born young people from a variety of cultural and ethnic backgrounds as well as children and adolescents from immigrant families. These youth often present special problems that may have an impact on assessments:

> In the United States, culturally and linguistically diverse groups may face (a) racism and discrimination, (b) poverty, (c) conflicts associated with acculturation and assimilation, especially when children begin to identify more closely with the majority culture and reject their ethnic culture, (d) problems in dealing with medical, educational, social, and law enforcement organizations, and (e) problems in using standard English. (Sattler & Hoge, 2006; p. 83)

These issues can affect the conduct of assessments with the youth. Establishing rapport and communication in the assessment situation can present problems because of conflicts in attitudes and beliefs. Families and youth from certain cultural and ethnic minorities may be suspicious of adults from the majority culture and collecting information from them can be difficult. These youth may come from families who have had negative experiences with authority figures. Assessors themselves may hold biased or stereotyped attitudes that interfere with positive interactions with the youth. It is sad to acknowledge that professionals in juvenile justice systems are not always free of cultural and ethnic prejudices.

Bias may exist in the assessment instruments and diagnostic criteria. Personality tests developed and validated for members of the majority culture may not be valid for members of ethnic minority groups. It has also been suggested that diagnostic criteria represented in systems such as DSM-IV-TR may be culturally biased (Bird, Yager, Staghezza Gould, Canino, & Rubio-Stipec, 1990). For example, hyperactivity–attention deficit disorder may be overdiagnosed in some cultural groups where very low levels of activity are expected.

Difficulty in understanding the language of the interviewer and the assessment tools can present obstacles. There is a real danger than an interviewer will misinterpret responses of a youth with a poor command of English or one using dialects not fully understood by the interviewer. Similarly, administering an English language personality test to a youth with poor English language skills is inappropriate and unethical.

In some cases, especially with immigrant youth, the language barrier may be so great that an interpreter must be used. However, this may also present difficulties. The interpreter may have difficulty in understanding the youth. For example, a Spanish interpreter may not understand a youth who speaks a regional dialect of Spanish. It is also possible that the interpreter will hold biases that distort translations. An interpreter from the same culture as the youth may be offended by the youth's attitudes and provide erroneous interpretations. For example, some Asian groups are hesitant to discuss sexual matters and may distort a youth's report of these activities.

Ethical guidelines having a bearing on the conduct of assessments with cultural and ethnic minorities will be discussed below. However, a number of courses of action to help guard against the operation of bias can be noted here. First, the use of standardized assessment tools and procedures, as long as they have been shown appropriate to the group in question, can help reduce the chances of biases operating. For example, the use of one of the standardized risk/need instruments discussed in chapter 3 will encourage the assessor to consider a broad range of characteristics and circumstances of the youth rather than to focus on a simplified stereotype.

BEST PRACTICE

Help safeguard against bias by

- using standardized assessment tools and procedure,
- learning about the group to which the youth belongs, and
- examining your own attitudes and beliefs.

Second, the assessor should be encouraged to become knowledgeable about the groups with which he is dealing. For example, where assessing children of families recently arrived as refugees, the assessor should make an effort to understand that group and the challenges being faced by those families and youth.

On a more general level the assessor should make an effort to examine her own attitudes and beliefs regarding the cultural and ethnic minorities being dealt with. The professional should not be asked to suspend all judgment; however, she should consider whether those attitudes and beliefs are unfairly affecting the youth before them. Too often professionals who are members of the majority culture simply impose the attitudes and values of that culture on others. This can seriously impede assessment and case management activities.

Evaluating the Measures

The importance of researching the reliability and validity of measures has already been stressed. Information about these properties will be available from manuals or guides accompanying the instrument and from a search of the research literature. Reference materials such as the *Mental Measurements Yearbook* (Geisinger, Spies, Carlson, & Plake, 2007) can also be an important source of psychometric information. Issues relating specifically to the validation of risk/need assessment instruments will be discussed in chapter 5.

4
chapter

Cost

The cost of test materials and their administration is also a factor to be considered in evaluating the suitability of measures. Psychological services are sometimes expensive, and it is important to weigh those costs against the potential benefits of using the services. However, research shows that following principles of best practice, including the use of standardized assessment procedures, can lead to significantly reduced levels of reoffending. The savings there will often offset the costs of the assessment.

Professional Expertise

Standardized assessment instruments and procedures require varying levels of training and experience, and this must be considered in planning the assessment. As we have seen, some of the tools can be used by professionals such as probation officers, youth workers, or teachers with some special training. In other cases, however, the assessments must be conducted by qualified mental health professionals such as psychiatrists or psychologists. All professionals involved in the assessment should have a thorough understanding of child and adolescent development. As indicated, the use of the assessment instruments and procedures should be continually monitored, with periodic retraining being provided to those using the measures. The issue of quality control will be addressed shortly.

Preparation for the Assessment

It is important for the examiner to enter the assessment with all of the materials necessary to conduct the assessment and with the capacity to administer the instruments in an efficient manner. This is true both when only a structured interview is to be conducted and when a range of assessment instruments will be used. Careful preparation also includes considering the order in which instruments or procedures will be employed. Should the process begin with the conduct of the interview or with the administration of the test materials where they are to be used? Is it better to review file information before the interview, or is it important to form impressions from the interview without exposure to potentially biasing information? In what order should youth, parents, and collaterals be interviewed? These issues should be resolved before the assessment begins.

BEST PRACTICE

Carefully prepare for the assessment, including planning which instruments or procedures will be used and in what order.

Careful planning for the assessment is important in two senses. First, the utility of the assessment depends very directly on the competent and consistent administration of instruments. This is particularly true of standardized tests where ineffective administration and scoring may render the results invalid. Second, inefficient or ineffective administration of the procedures may interfere with the relationship established with the examinee and somehow distort information collected from them. This issue is addressed more fully next.

Quality Control

Developing policies and procedures to ensure appropriate uses of the assessment measures is critical (Andrews & Dowden, 2005). As noted, professional expertise is critical to the success of any assessment effort. Some measure of quality control is available in the case of professional mental health workers. The professional and regulatory bodies of psychologists and psychiatrists discussed above provide established guidelines for their respective educational programs and procedures for monitoring the activities of the professionals. In some cases these monitoring procedures have the force of law.

The situation is somewhat different for non-mental-health professionals engaged in conducting violence risk and need assessments for pretrial detention, alternative measures, or disposition/commitment decisions. This includes probation officers, social workers, and youth workers. The best-practice research discussed earlier suggests that these assessments are improved where based on the standardized broad-based risk/needs measures. In this case it is the responsibility of the agency to ensure that adequate training and

BEST PRACTICE

Recommended steps for introducing and managing new assessment procedures into an organization:

- Include a commitment to the use of standardized assessments in the agency's mission statement.
- Provide all relevant administrative and judicial personnel with an introduction to the procedures.
- Integrate the new procedures into the system in a judicious manner; avoid duplication of effort.
- Provide comprehensive training in the procedures to all personnel who will be conducting the assessments.
- Ensure resource personnel are available to answer questions about the procedures and monitor their use.
- Provide periodic retraining and reliability checks.
- Periodically evaluate the benefits of using the procedures.

monitoring procedures are in place. Most of the broad-based instruments described above are accompanied by training programs for instructing officers in administration, scoring, and interpretation of the measures. See the Best Practice box for a review of efforts that are essential to ensure that assessments are conducted effectively.

Data Collection | 5

T his chapter provides discussions of topics relevant to the data collection phase of the assessment. This includes a review of general issues in the conduct of assessments, guidelines for the interview process, and the assessment context.

General Issues in the Conduct of Assessments

Chapter 4 provided a discussion of some practical considerations in the selection of assessment instruments and procedures. This included topics relating to the relevance of measures, bases for evaluating measures, cost considerations, and professional expertise in the conduct of assessments. The following sections extend that discussion to include more general issues in the conduct of assessments.

Establishing Rapport

An important practical concern is the type of rapport established with the examinee. There may be therapeutic or counseling situations where the goal is to observe the examinee under conditions of anger or stress. Generally, though, the intention is to put the examinee at ease and to collect information under the most natural conditions possible.

Anyone with experience in working with adolescents knows that establishing a positive relationship is often problematic. Most adolescents enter an assessment situation with a friendly and cooperative attitude; however, there are cases where the youth's approach is hostile, suspicious, resistant, or withdrawn. These attitudes are

BEST PRACTICE

As part of the assessment

- Establish a good rapport with the youth
- Carefully observe the youth
- Integrate information from multiple sources

often particularly pronounced in young people with serious behavioral or emotional problems as is true of many youthful offenders. Also, many offenders have had what they perceive to be negative treatment by authorities, and this complicates the conduct of the interview. Finally, the client may have committed very brutal acts that are difficult to deal with. It often takes a very skilled assessor to deal with these difficult youth.

A sensitivity to potential dynamics of the examiner–youth relationship is important. A young female who has experienced serious abuse from a middle-aged male may not be entirely comfortable with an examiner who reminds her of the abuser. There may also be differing styles among assessors that could be considered in matching professional with client. For example, some probation officers are comfortable dealing with hostile and aggressive youth, and others work more effectively with lower-risk clients. Special problems in dealing with minority group youth will be dealt with shortly. There is often little choice in who conducts the assessment and we may not consider it appropriate for the client to select his assessor. Still, establishing a relationship of mutual trust and respect is the ideal in the assessment situation. Some guides in conducting the assessment interview will be discussed below.

Observing the Youth

Careful observation of the youth during the assessment process is important in two respects. Signs of increasing frustration, anger, fatigue, or distraction may call for a change in the procedure. Second, the observations may be important in the formation of the final assessment or diagnosis. Primary dependence should be placed on the standardized assessments, but the informal observations are often important from the point of view of filling in gaps or suggesting the need for additional assessments.

Integrating Information from Multiple Sources

Ideally, data should be collected from multiple sources. This includes interview information from the youth and possibly interview information from parents and other collaterals such as teachers, clinicians, and police officers. It may also include file information and, where a psychological assessment is conducted, test scores. Integrating this information to produce a prediction of the likelihood of future violence and a case management plan is sometimes difficult. It requires evaluating the reliability of information collected from different sources and resolving conflicting information. The integration of the information can be aided by the use of one of the standardized risk/need assessment tools described below. However, the process still relies on the skill of the assessor.

Guidelines for the Interview Process

Assessments conducted in juvenile justice systems for any purpose will necessarily involve an interview with the youth and, where feasible, collateral sources such as parents, teachers, or professionals associated with the youth. Highly structured interview schedules such as the Diagnostic Interview Schedule for Children (Shaffer, 1996) were described in the previous chapter. Comprehensive risk/need instruments such as the Washington State Juvenile Court Assessment and YLS/CMI described earlier also provide semistructured interview schedules to assist in collecting information required for completing the inventories. Because research has shown that structured and standardized instruments are superior to more informal assessment procedures, either fully structured or semistructured interview formats should be employed.

It should be understood that the interview can also be viewed as part of the therapeutic or counseling process where the assessor has an opportunity to provide interventions to the youth. This would not be the case, of course, where the assessment is conducted for purely forensic purposes.

The interview can play a particularly important role in initial dealings with highly unmotivated and resistant youth, a pattern frequently observed in youth who have engaged in serious and violent crimes. Miller and Rollnick's (2002) motivational interviewing program provides valuable guidelines for the conduct of the interview and for using the interview as a counseling device. It is a valuable resource for helping people improve their interviewing skills. This program emphasizes the importance of expressing empathy, utilizing resistance, and supporting self-efficacy. Rather than simply confronting the youth with their transgressions and failures, the goal is to encourage them to move toward more positive attitudes and behaviors. This is sometimes a great challenge with

Table 5.1 | Guidelines for Interviewing

- **Establish rapport:** Dealing with antisocial youth is sometimes challenging, but it is our responsibility as professionals to treat the client with respect and to make every attempt to gain his trust. Expressing empathy for the client's situation will often help in establishing a relationship.

- **Listen carefully:** Eliciting good information from a client depends on listening carefully to what she has to say. It is important to enter the interview with an open mind rather than with an agenda imposed on the youth. Too often youth's complaint that adults never listen to what they have to say is justified.

- **Remain objective:** The interviewer should maintain a positive attitude and treat the youth's responses in a respectful manner; however, this does not necessarily mean that the interviewer endorses the youth's responses. It is possible to challenge the youth's beliefs in a positive manner.

- **Facilitate communication:** There is little point in using language or concepts the youth does not understand; ensure that questions and responses are clearly understood by the client.

- **Maintain control:** The youth should be treated with consideration during the interview, but not be allowed to direct or divert the questioning.

- **Avoid argumentation:** Engaging the youth in lengthy arguments and confronting any of the youth's positions in a hostile manner is usually counterproductive. Maintain a positive atmosphere as much as possible.

Note: Adapted from Clinical and Forensic Interviewing of Children and Families: Guidelines for the Mental Health, Education, Pediatric, and Child Maltreatment Fields, by J. M. Sattler, 1998, San Diego, CA: Sattler Publishing Company; Assessment of Children: Behavioral, Social, and Clinical Foundations (5th ed.), by J. M. Sattler and R. D. Hoge, 2006, San Diego, CA: Sattler Publishing Company.

serious and violent offenders, but the approach is more effective than one based exclusively on confrontation and argumentation.

Other resources for assisting in developing interview skills are provided by Sattler (1998) and Sattler and Hoge (2006). Table 5.1 list some general guidelines derived from those sources.

As indicated in chapter 5, special interviewing skills may be required in dealing with youth from cultural or ethnic minority groups or those with language deficits. Sattler (1998) and Sattler and Hoge (2006) have provided a full discussion of that issue.

Assessment Context

Another issue concerns the setting in which the assessment is to be conducted. This depends to some extent on the purpose of the assessment. Where the assessment is conducted for the purpose of contributing to decisions regarding legal issues such as waivers or transfers or appreciation of *Miranda* rights, the assessment will likely be conducted by a psychologist or psychiatrist within a juvenile justice or mental health facility.

Where the assessment is conducted for placement or disposition planning purposes, it will likely be conducted by a mental health or juvenile justice professional within a juvenile justice facility. This would be the case, for example, where a probation officer conducts a risk and need assessment as part of a disposition report.

Assessment Centers

The use of assessment centers for evaluating youth at intake presents a special situation. The Office of Juvenile Justice and Delinquency Prevention (Oldenettel & Wordes, 2000) has developed the Community Assessment Center concept as part of the larger Comprehensive Strategy for Serious, Violent, and Chronic Juvenile Offenders (Wilson & Howell, 1995). The following are the main features of the assessment center concept as it would be applied within a community or region:

- A single point of entry is provided for all juveniles who come into contact with the juvenile justice system.

- An immediate and comprehensive assessment is provided. This may involve an initial screening process and then a more intensive assessment for those identified as moderate or high risk/need.
- A management information system is created to monitor the youth's needs and their progress through the system.
- An integrated case management system uses "information from the assessment process and the management information system to develop recommendations, facilitate access to services, conduct follow-ups, and periodically reassess youth" (Oldenettel & Wordes, 2000, p. 2).

Ideally, such an assessment center would also coordinate with services provided to the youth by the educational, mental health, and social service systems in order to avoid the fragmentation of services so often observed in our communities.

The assessment center concept is a useful one because it encourages the conduct of careful intake assessments. However, care should be exercised. First, it is important to ensure clear communication between the assessment unit and those who will be developing and implementing case plans. Second, and related, those involved in case planning and management should be involved in the assessment process. In too many cases, there is poor integration between the assessment and case planning/delivery processes. Finally, it must be remembered that youth change over time and that the initial assessment may require revisions as circumstances change.

Review of Standardized Instruments and Procedures Relevant to Risk/Need Assessments

A variety of standardized and clinical instruments and procedures are available for assisting in assessing and managing risks and needs in forensic settings. Relatively few of these have been designed specifically for evaluating risk and need factors associated with serious and violent offending. However, they can provide assistance in evaluating risk, needs, responsivity, and protective factors relevant to such evaluations. Instruments and procedures developed for general application will be discussed first, followed by measures specifically devised for forensic assessments. Use of the measures in formal reports will be discussed in chapters 6 and 7.

General Application Measures

A wide range of standardized personality and attitude measures are available for use as part of an assessment of risk, need, responsivity, and protective factors associated with serious and violent criminal activity. Though these have not been specifically developed for forensic assessments or validated for these purposes, they are capable of yielding information about emotional and behavioral functioning relevant to the risk and need factors associated with violent offending. Detailed reviews of these measures are available from Hoge (1999b), Hoge and Andrews (1996), and Sattler and Hoge (2006), and only a sample of relevant measures will be included in this discussion.

PERSONALITY TESTS

These tests can form an important part of an evaluation of a youth's propensity for violence and can contribute to case planning and management activities. For example, the Minnesota Multiphasic Personality Inventory—Adolescent (MMPI-A; Butcher et al., 1992) yields scores on dimensions potentially relevant to evaluations of risk for violence. Three patterns of scores on the MMPI-A are commonly observed in juvenile offenders: Psychopathic Deviate–Hypomania, Psychopathic Deviate–Paranoia, and Depression–Psychopathic Deviate.

Special mention should also be made of the Psychopathy Checklist—Youth Version (PCL-YV; Forth et al., 2003). This instrument is sometimes used as a risk/need assessment tool, although it is primarily designed for evaluating the presence of psychopathic traits. Although the instrument has shown value in predicting violent actions (Forth, 2005), questions have been raised about the ethics of using the instrument as well as the construct of

5
chapter

Table 5.2 | Examples of Standardized Personality Tests Useful in Forensic Assessments

Test	Reference
Adolescent Psychopathology Scale	Reynolds (1998)
Jesness Inventory—Revised	Jesness (2003)
Millon Adolescent Clinical Inventory	Millon (1993)
Minnesota Multiphasic Personality Inventory—Adolescent	Butcher et al. (1992)
Personality Inventory for Youth	Lachar and Gruber (1995)
Psychopathy Checklist—Youth Version	Forth et al. (2003)

psychopathy with adolescents (see Edens et al., 2001; Seagrave & Grisso, 2002). The instrument may have use in evaluating dimensions associated with violent actions (e.g., lack of empathy, egocentrism), but the measure should not be used to diagnose or label youth as psychopaths.

Table 5.2 identifies a number of personality tests potentially useful in assessments of a propensity for serious and violent crime. However, it has to be emphasized that the utility of these measures for assessing and managing risk for serious and violent criminal activity has not been directly established. Scores from the measures may be useful in developing intervention programs for violent youth, but the scores cannot be used as a sole basis to establish risk for engaging in these actions. Normally, a standardized personality test would form one part of a comprehensive forensic evaluation. Administration and interpretation of these instruments is generally conducted by a mental health professional with special training in use of the instrument.

BEWARE
Personality tests are not adequate in themselves to establish risk of violence in juveniles.

STANDARDIZED INTERVIEW SCHEDULES

The interview can be conducted according to completely unstructured, semistructured, or structured procedures. Research noted above indicates that the validity of information collection increases where structured or standardized assessment procedures are used, and this applies particularly to the interview process. Table 5.3 identifies a number of structured interview schedules potentially useful in collecting information about risk, need, responsivity, and protective considerations associated with violence assessments.

Some of these schedules are specifically designed to yield DSM diagnoses. An example is the Diagnostic Interview Schedule for Children (DISC; Shaffer, 1996). This is capable of yielding the full range of diagnoses relevant to children and youth, including Conduct Disorder and Oppositional—Defiant Disorder.

The Child and Adolescent Functional Assessment Scale (CAFAS; Hodges, 2000) is another example of an interview schedule relevant to assessing and managing risk in serious offenders. The instrument was originally developed for evaluating risk for serious emotional disturbance. Subscales of the measure reflect the youth's degree of adjustment in various areas of life (see Table 5.4).

Use of these standardized interview schedules generally do not require an advanced degree but training in their application is

Table 5.3 | Examples of Standardized and Semistructured Interview Schedules

Measure	Reference
Adolescent Diagnostic Interview	Winters and Henley (1993)
Child and Adolescent Functional Assessment Scale	Hodges (2000)
Diagnostic Interview for Children and Adolescents	Reich (2000)
Diagnostic Interview Schedule for Children	Shaffer (1996)

5
chapter

Table 5.4 | Scales of the Child and Adolescent Functional Assessment Scale

Role performance
School/work
Home
Community
Behavior toward others
Moods
Moods/emotions
Self-harmful behavior
Substance abuse
Thinking

Note: *Child and Adolescent Functional Assessment Scale*, by K. Hodges, 2000, Ypsilanti, MI: Eastern Michigan University

required. Further, it is important to pay close attention to the careful conduct of the interview. Sattler (1998) and Sattler and Hoge (2006) provide more detailed discussions of these schedules.

CHECKLIST AND RATING INSTRUMENTS

Standardized rating and checklist measures are often useful in collecting information for risk and management assessments. These may serve as screening tools for the preliminary identification of problems or as part of more intensive psychological assessments. Some of these are self-report measures completed by the youth, and others are completed by parents, teachers, or others involved with the youth. Many of these measures can be administered and

BEWARE
Obtain training in the application of standardized interview schedules before using them with youth.

Table 5.5 | Examples of Rating/Checklist Measures Useful in Forensic Assessments

Measure	Reference
Antisocial Process Screening Device	Frick and Hare (2001)
Child Behavior Checklist (Teacher, Parent, Self-report versions)	Achenbach and Rescorla (2001)
Conners' Rating Scales—Revised	Conners (1997)
Devereux Scales of Mental Disorder	Naglieri, LeBuffe, and Pfeiffer (1994)
Massachusetts Youth Screening Instrument—2	Grisso and Barnum (2000)
Problem-Oriented Screening Instrument for Teenagers	Rahdert (1991)
Revised Behavior Problem Checklist	Quay and Peterson (1996)

scored by non-mental-health professionals such as teachers or probation officers. However, some background in the basics of assessment as well as training in the use of the specific measure is usually required. Table 5.5 identifies a number of these instruments relevant to assessment and case management of serious juvenile offenders. Information from these measures is of primary value in describing characteristics of the youth that may be relevant to the development of predictions of violence. Two will be briefly described for illustrative purposes.

The MAYSI-2 (Grisso & Barnum, 2003) is a self-report screening measure designed to detect symptoms of mental and emotional disturbance. The instrument is frequently used in juvenile justice systems as a preliminary indicator of mental health problems. Subscores include Alcohol/Drug Use, Depressed/Anxious, and Suicide Ideation. Where potential problems are indicated, more thorough assessments are required.

The parent, teacher, clinician, and youth forms of the CBCL (Achenbach & Rescorla, 2001) have proven useful in identifying behavioral, emotional, and social problems in children and adolescents. The instrument is scored in terms of age- and gender-specific norms. Many of the behavioral dimensions assessed by this measure are relevant for evaluating risk and need factors associated with a propensity for violent offending (e.g., Attention Problems, Rule Breaking Behavior, Aggressive Behavior).

The instruments identified in Table 5.5 are all well standardized and supported by psychometric research. These measures can be especially useful because of their relative ease of administration and low cost. However, as with all psychological measures, administration and interpretation must be done with care.

Forensic Assessment Instruments: Attitudes

Several standardized self-report measures of antisocial attitudes, values, and beliefs are also available for use with adolescents (Table 5.6). The HITQ (Gibbs et al., 2001) has already been described as a

Table 5.6 Measures of Antisocial Attitudes, Values, and Beliefs

Measure	Reference
Attitudes Toward Institutional Authority	Gordon (1993)
Criminal Sentiments Scale—Modified	Simourd (1997)
Criminal Thinking Scales	Knight, Garner, Simpson, Morey, and Flynn (2006)
Hostile Interpretations Questionnaire	Simourd and Mamuza (2002)
How I Think Questionnaire	Gibbs et al. (2001)
Pride in Delinquency Scale	Shields and Whitehall (1991)
Revised Legal Attitudes Questionnaire	Kravitz, Cutler, and Brock (1993)

measure of antisocial attitudes and dysfunctional thinking. The important role of antisocial attitudes, values, and beliefs was discussed in chapter 3. The careful assessment of these is important in any effort to evaluate risk for serious and violent delinquency.

BEST PRACTICE

Use standardized measures of antisocial attitudes, values, and beliefs as part of the assessment.

Forensic Assessment Instruments: Broad-Based Risk/Need Measures

Comprehensive or broad-based risk/need assessment instruments constitute an important category of measures for assessing risk for serious and violent criminal activity and for identifying needs relevant to case planning and management activities. The earlier instruments of this type were limited because they were based on a limited range of static risk factors such as age at first arrest, number of prior convictions, or severity of the offense, whereas more recent instruments have been built on the growing body of research on risk and need factors discussed in chapter 4 (Borum & Verhaagen, 2006; Hoge, 1999a; Hoge & Andrews, 1996; Le Blanc, 1998).

Some of the measures discussed below can be characterized as actuarial instruments in that they yield empirically based estimates of risk and need. Other measures in this category represent a structured professional judgment approach. Some have been specifically developed for assessing risk for violent offending, but all have been shown valid in predicting both general and serious offending. These instruments are of value in helping to synthesize a range of information about the client and in guiding decisions about appropriate community or residential placements, levels of supervision, and appropriate interventions. The strengths and limitations of these measures will be noted in this section and discussed in more detail in chapter 6.

All of the instruments described below are in the form of structured checklists or interview schedules, and all are accompanied by detailed manuals and scoring keys. Completion of the instruments is based on file review and interview data and any other information available about the youth. Table 5.7 provides a

5
chapter

Table 5.7 | Comprehensive Risk/Needs Assessment Instruments

Measure	Reference
Arizona Juvenile Risk Assessment Form	Ashford, LeCroy, and Bond-Maupin (1986)
Early Assessment Risk Lists for Boys and Girls	Augimeri, Koegl, Webster, and Levene (2001); Levene et al. (2001)
Estimate of Risk of Adolescent Sexual Offense Recidivism	Worling and Curwen (2000)
Juvenile Probation and Aftercare Assessment Form	Baird (1984, 1985)
Structured Assessment of Violence Risk in Youth	Borum et al. (2005)
Washington State Juvenile Court Risk Assessment	Barnoski (2004)
Youth Level of Service/Case Management Inventory	Hoge and Andrews (2002)

listing of comprehensive risk/need assessment instruments potentially relevant to risk assessment and management activities. Five of these measures will be discussed in some detail to illustrate this important category of measures.

ERASOR

The Estimate of Risk of Adolescent Sexual Offense Recidivism—2 (ERASOR; Worling & Curwen, 2001) is an example of a structured clinical assessment tool focusing specifically on adolescent sexual offending. It is designed to evaluate risk for sexual reoffending on the part of individuals who have previously committed a sexual assault and to offer guidance in the development of treatment strategies.

Twenty-five risk factors are included in the ERASOR. Examples include "deviant sexual interest," "ever sexually assaulted two or more victims," and "antisocial interpersonal orientation." A specific scoring algorithm is not provided. Instead, the assessor categorizes the level of risk as low, moderate, or high, based on the total number of items checked and the assessor's judgments about the pattern of risk observed.

Limited reliability and validity information are currently available for the measure. Guidelines for administering and scoring the instrument are available, as is a specialized training program. The authors emphasize the importance of utilizing multiple sources of information in scoring items. The measure is appropriate for use by non-mental-health professionals with special training.

SAVRY

The *Structured Assessment of Violence Risk in Youth* (SAVRY; Borum, Bartel, & Forth, 2005) provides for the structured clinical assessment of risk for violent actions. Items in the scale are empirically derived and specifically focused in adolescents.

The 24 risk items are divided into three categories: Historical (e.g., "history of violence"), Individual (e.g., "negative attitudes"), and Social/Contextual (e.g., "poor parental management"). Six items describing Protective Factors are also included (e.g., "strong social support"). Scoring is based on a Summary Risk rating of low, moderate, or high. An algorithm for calculating this is not provided; rather, the score is arrived at by the assessor based on her professional judgment.

Psychometric support for the instrument has been summarized by Borum et al. (2005). Two investigations reporting support for inter-rater reliability are reviewed; a number of studies reporting significant levels of concurrent and predictive validity are also reported. The latter include demonstrations that SAVRY scores are predictive of general and violent offending.

Unlike the other comprehensive risk/need instruments described in this section, use of the SAVRY does not require special training. The authors indicate that a familiarity with the manual is sufficient.

WSJCA

The Washington State Juvenile Court Assessment (WSJCA; Barnoski, 2004; Barnoski & Markussen, 2005) is part of a two-step assessment process in which a short screening instrument is first

Table 5.8 | Domains from the Washington State Juvenile Court Assessment

Criminal History	Demographics
School	Use of Free Time
Employment	Relationships
Family	Alcohol and Drugs
Mental Health	Attitudes/Behaviors
Aggression	Skills

Note: *Assessing Risk for Re-offense: Validating the Washington State Juvenile Court Assessment* (Report No. 04-03-1201), by R. Barnoski, 2004, Olympia, WA: Washington State Institute for Public Policy.

administered. Youth who obtain a moderate- or high-risk score on that scale are then administered the full WSJCA. Only the latter instrument is discussed here.

The 132-item WSJCA provides for assessing both static and dynamic risk factors within 12 domains (see Table 5.8). Four types of scores are produced: Static Risk, Dynamic Risk, Static Protective, and Dynamic Protective. The scoring is designed to evaluate the youth's level of risk for reoffending and to identify need and protective factors relevant to case planning and management. High-, moderate-, and low-risk ranges are based on the total and domain scores. In this sense the instrument can be considered an actuarial measure.

Barnoski and Markussen (2005) have summarized the available reliability and validity evidence relevant to the measure. Adequate levels of internal consistency are reported, but evidence is not presented regarding the inter-rater reliability or validity of the full assessment instrument.

Administration and scoring of the measure does require an intensive training program, although an advanced degree in a mental health field is not required.

Table 5.9 | Components of the Youth Level of Service/Case Management Inventory

Part I	Assessment of Risks and Needs
Part II	Summary of Risk/Need Factors
Part III	Assessment of Other Needs/Special Considerations
Part IV	Professional Override
Part V	Contact Level
Part VI	Case Management Plan

Note: *Youth Level of Service/Case Management Inventory User's Manual,* by R. D. Hoge and D. A. Andrews, 2002, North Tonawanda, NY: Multi-Health Systems.

YLS/CMI

The YLS/CMI (Hoge, 2005; Hoge & Andrews, 2002) is a standardized actuarial measure that provides estimates of risk for reoffending and a framework for developing case plans based on the risk/needs assessment. It also includes a professional override provision to allow the examiner discretion in identifying the level of risk. Table 5.9 outlines the six parts of the measure.

The first section of the YLS/CMI includes 42 items reflecting characteristics of the offender (e.g., "chronic drug use") or his circumstances (e.g., "parent provides inadequate supervision") identified in the literature as correlates of juvenile offending. The items are divided into the following subscales: Prior and Current Offenses/Dispositions, Family Circumstances/Parenting, Education/Employment, Peer Relations, Substance Abuse, Leisure/Recreation, Personality/Behavior, and Attitudes/ Orientation. An opportunity is also provided for indicating areas of strength. Subsequent sections include Summary of Risks and Needs, Assessment of Other Needs and Special Considerations, Professional Override, Contact Level, and Case Management

5
chapter

Plan. The Case Management Plan involves identifying a set of goals reflecting the risk/needs assessment and identification of means of achieving those goals.

The instrument can be used as a structured professional judgment procedure or actuarial procedure. In the latter case, low, moderate, high, and very high ranges for total and subscales are based on empirical data. Risk scores can also be expressed as *T-scores* based on normative data.

Hoge (2005) has reviewed current psychometric information for the YLS/CMI. Satisfactory levels of internal consistency and inter-rater reliability have been reported. Construct- and criterion-related (concurrent and predictive) validity support have also been presented. Predictive validity has been demonstrated for boys and girls, some minority groupings (African American and Canadian Aboriginal), and various national settings.

The YLS/CMI is designed for use by mental health professionals and by other juvenile justice and correctional professionals (e.g., probation officers, youth officers) with training in administration and interpretation of the measure.

ADDITIONAL COMMENTS ON BROAD-BASED RISK/NEED MEASURES

Brief summaries of psychometric research on the measures have been presented above. Meta-analyses of validation research on selected risk/need instruments have been reported by Edens, Campbell, and Weir (2007) and Schwalbe (2007, 2008). The Buros *Mental Measurements Yearbooks* also represent a potential source of information regarding some of the measures. However, a search of the empirical literature should be conducted when selecting a measure for a specific situation and purpose. It is particularly important to ensure that reliability and validity support is available for the age, gender, and cultural/ethnic group membership of the youth.

BEST PRACTICE

Conduct a search of the empirical literature to select a measure specific to the youth's case.

Semi-structured interview
> Youth Level of Service/Case Management Inventory Interview Schedule
> (Hoge & Andrews, 2002)

Cognitive Aptitude and Achievement Measures
> Wechsler Intelligence Scale for Children–IV (Wechsler, 2004)
> Kaufman Test of Educational Achievement (Kaufman & Kaufman, 1985)

Personality Test
> Minnesota Multiphasic Personality Inventory–Adolescent (Butcher et al., 1992)

Rating Measures of Behavioral Pathology
> Child Behavior Checklist–Parent Version (Achenbach & Rescorla, 2001)
> Child Behavior Checklist–Teacher Report Form (Achenbach & Rescorla, 2001)

Broad-Based Risk/Needs Assessment Measure
> Youth Level of Service/Case Management Inventory (Hoge & Andrews, 2002)

Figure 5.1   Example of an Assessment Battery for a Comprehensive
Risk/Needs Assessment

Forensic Assessment Measures: Example of a Comprehensive Assessment Battery

Assessments are conducted for a wide variety of purposes in forensic settings. In many cases, all that is needed is an intake interview and completion of a standardized risk/need assessment tool to establish the youth's level of risk and areas of treatment needed. These assessments can be conducted by a probation officer or other court official with training in the use of a standardized instrument such as the WSJCA or YLS/CMI. In other cases, however, a comprehensive mental health assessment by a psychologist or psychiatrist is required. This would be the case, for example, where forensic decisions regarding competence to stand trial or consent to understand *Miranda* warnings are required or where serious behavioral or emotional problems exist that might affect decisions about the youth.

Figure 5.1 presents an example of a comprehensive assessment battery that might be used for offering guidance to a judge in making a disposition or sentencing decision regarding a special needs youth. The battery could yield information on risk for general and violent offending and about treatment needs that might be addressed in a disposition.

5
chapter

Interpretation | 6

T he goal of violence risk and management exercises is to produce an estimate of the likelihood the youth will engage in violent actions in the future and to provide information that can be used to develop a case management plan for reducing this risk. Achieving these goals involves collecting information regarding risk, need, responsivity, and protective factors and interpreting the information to yield estimates of risk and management needs. This chapter focuses on the interpretation phase of the process.

The assessment of risk for violence will be guided by a specific purpose within the forensic context. The assessment may be required for a decision regarding sentence or disposition, the level of security to be provided in a detention or custody setting, the intensity of supervision in a probation order, or, reflecting an important principle of best practice, the intensity of the intervention provided to the youth. The latter will form part of the case planning and management decision. Although the general rules governing the risk assessment are common across decision areas, the specifics may vary somewhat. For example, it may be important to indicate the kinds of situations provoking violent responses when making management decisions in a custody setting.

The Role of Judgments in the Assessment Process

The use of subjective judgments in the assessment process is an important issue. Purely clinical or unstructured assessments depend on a subjective interpretation of information collected in interviews and possibly through other sources such as test scores or file reviews. For example, a probation officer asked to make an estimate of risk for violence relating to a pretrial detention decision might interview the youth and collaterals (parents, police), review the youth's record, and, on the basis of her experience, form a subjective judgment that the youth is high or low risk for committing a violent act.

Although there is variability in the reliability and validity of unstructured clinical assessments, they are generally less psychometrically sound than standardized assessment procedures such as actuarial and structured professional judgment assessments. However, even in the latter cases interpretative judgments are required. In the case of actuarial assessments, the formula or algorithm specifies the factors to be considered, synthesizes the information, and produces an interpretation reflecting a level of risk. The formula may be based simply on the total number of risk items checked or may be more complicated when items are differentially weighted. However, it is important to remember that the information entered into the formula may be based on the interpretation. For example, an item such as "substance abuse interferes with life" calls for a judgment on the part of the examiner. Thus, although a high degree of structure is represented in the choice of factors and in the final synthesis of information, subjective judgments are still involved at an earlier point in the process.

Structured professional judgment assessments present a somewhat complicated picture. This method requires the examiner to collect information about potential risk, need, responsivity, and protective factors and then produce a summary statement of risk and need (e.g., high risk for reoffending, high level of need). The method differs from the clinical method because the collection of information is structured, generally in the form of a checklist. This is designed to provide guidance to the information collection phase of the process. However, interpretative judgments are still involved in the process. An item such as "high levels of anger" calls for a judgment on the part of the examiner. Further, other types of assessment such as personality tests or attitude ratings may be used to assist in scoring items, and those measures often require a measure of judgment on the part of the examiner. Finally, the final translation of the information into a summary statement depends on the subjective judgment of the examiner.

Although a certain level of subjective judgment is involved in actuarial and structured professional judgment assessments, research discussed earlier indicates that these more standardized procedures are superior to unstructured clinical assessments.

Alternative Scoring Formats

The description of characteristics of individuals forms the basis for psychological assessments. In some cases these descriptions are qualitative in nature. For example, the individual is described as gifted, autistic, or high risk for violent offending. In other cases the descriptions are quantitative. For example, the individual is characterized in terms of the relative amount of intelligence displayed, the degree of attention deficit disorder, or the probability of engaging in a criminal act. Descriptions or diagnoses yielded by clinical or structured professional assessments are generally qualitative in nature, whereas those yielded by standardized and actuarial measures may be qualitative or quantitative.

Qualitative Descriptions
Qualitative descriptions are often a useful means for summarizing and conveying information about individuals. Diagnosing a youth as attention-deficit-disordered or at high risk for committing a violent act provides information about behavioral characteristics of the youth and can help guide treatment efforts.

Most assessments of violence risk are based on a structured professional judgment procedure and most yield *categorical indices*. In the simplest case youths are categorized as high risk or not high risk. In other cases multiple risk categories are used. For example, the SAVRY measure requires the examiner to characterize the youth as low, moderate, or high risk for violent offending based on the information collected through the instrument. The YLS/CMI yields four risk categories: low, moderate, high, and very high risk. In this case total risk score ranges are provided to guide the categorization.

6
chapter

However, problems sometimes arise in the use of these risk level categories (Achenbach, 1995; Grisso & Appelbaum, 1992; Scotti, Morris, McNeil, & Hawkins, 1996). Unless there is a solid research foundation for the categorizations, questions of validity can be raised. What is the actual meaning of a diagnosis of high risk and what specific implications does it have for future behavior and for interventions? Psychometric data supporting the predictive validity of most of the broad-based risk/needs assessment tools described in chapter 6 have been presented. It has been demonstrated, for example, that the risk categories associated with the SAVRY and YLS/CMI are predictive of future antisocial behavior. However, as discussed above, this research is still somewhat limited in the range of samples studied. The issue of validity is explored further later in this chapter.

Quantitative Descriptions

The second type of scoring format involves quantitative scores expressed relative to a point on an underlying continuum. These scores can be arrived at in one of two ways: *criterion-referenced* or *normative-referenced*. Criterion-referenced assessments express scores relative to behavioral or performance markers. For example, a youth exhibiting 6 out of 10 symptoms of conduct disorder would receive a score of 60%. Measures of risk and need are often scored in this manner. That is, the degree of risk is expressed relative to a percentage of risk markers. Although there may be some theoretical justification for these indices, it is also essential to present empirical data supporting the actual validity of the risk estimates.

Normative-referenced scoring is based on a comparison of an individual's score with aggregate scores from a sample of individuals. Standardized individual intelligence tests illustrate the procedure. Raw scores on the measure are interpreted with reference to a normative sample, such that, for example, a WISC-4 score of 100 means that the individual's raw score matched that of the average of the comparison normative sample. A variety of procedures for calculating normative-referenced scores are available (see Hoge, 1999b; Sattler & Hoge, 2006).

Most standardized personality and rating/checklist behavioral measures utilize normative-referenced scoring. For example, scores from the CBCL can be expressed as T-scores calculated with reference to a normative sample. To illustrate, a T-score of 60 on one of the scales would indicate that the youth's score fell at 1 *SD* above the mean relative to the standardization sample.

Some of the broad-based risk/needs scores discussed in chapter 6 can also be scored in this way. For example, raw scores from the YLS/CMI can be expressed as T-scores based on a sample of juvenile offenders. To illustrate, a total T-score of 50 would indicate that the total number of risk/need items for the youth was equal to the average number of risk factors for a sample of offenders. The utility of these standard scores depends, as we saw earlier, on the relevance of the standardization sample to the youth being assessed.

Some of the risk/needs measures for adults also yield concrete actuarial scores. That is, scores from the measures can be translated into actual estimates of the probability of reoffending. For example, total scores from the LS/CMI can be expressed as a probability of committing another criminal act over a specified period of time. These scores are based on empirical data linking scores from the measure with the actual incidence of reoffending. However, none of the existing broad-based risk/needs measures for youth permit this type of scoring.

Computer-Based Scoring and Interpretation

Computers have been widely used for some time in collecting and recording responses to tests and other measures. Many of the self-report personality tests and rating/checklist measures can be administered through a computer. Also, examiners can often record interview responses and checklist responses directly into the computer. Some mention should also be made of the use of computer-based scoring and the interpretation of assessment measures. Computers have had a significant impact on the assessment process (see Hoge, 1999b; Sattler & Hoge, 2006), and their impact is likely to grow in the future.

6
chapter

Computer-Based Scoring

Computer software has also been used for some time in calculating scores from raw data. There are now computer programs available for scoring a wide range of standardized tests, rating scales, and checklists. For example, several programs are available for calculating standardized scores for the WISC-4. These yield the full-scale, verbal, and performance IQ scores, various subtest scores, and a variety of profile and other specialized scores. Some of the broad-based risk/needs assessment instruments discussed in chapter 4 offer computer software programs to assist in scoring the instruments. These computer scoring programs have the advantages of eliminating the tedious clerical work often involved in the scoring of instruments and of improving scoring accuracy.

Computer-Based Interpretations

Another type of computer development involves computer-based interpretations. In this case the computer program yields not only the scores from the measuring instrument but also an interpretation of the scores. In some cases this involves providing an assessment or diagnosis as well as programming recommendations. One of the earliest efforts to develop a computer-based test interpretation was in connection with the MMPI in the early 1960s. That has led to similar efforts with other standardized measures of personality and psychopathology, intelligence, and achievement. None of the broad-based risk/needs assessment instruments discussed earlier provide computer-based interpretations; however, some of the personality tests and behavioral checklist/rating measures presented in chapter 4 do offer such software.

Although computer-based interpretations have become widely available and very popular, their use has aroused considerable controversy (see Garb, 2000; Matarazzo, 1992). The major criticism relates to lack of validity information for the computer-based interpretations. Psychometric information may be

BEWARE
The use of computer-based interpretation is controversial.

available for the assessment tools underlying the interpretations, but such is usually not the case for the interpretations themselves. This problem is compounded by the fact that the interpretations are often made available to individuals without the training and knowledge to utilize them effectively. The ethical issues raised by computer-based interpretations have received considerable attention by professional groups (e.g., American Educational Research Association, American Psychological Association, & National Council on Measurement in Education, 1999; American Psychological Association, 1986), but the issues have not been resolved.

The Validity of Risk Assessments

The validity of assessments underlying the violence risk predictions has an important bearing on the interpretation of the assessments. Two forms of validity discussed earlier have particular relevance to violence risk assessments: construct validity and criterion-related predictive validity.

Construct Validity

The first, construct validity, refers to the theoretical meaning of a measure. It can also be defined in terms of the accuracy of a measure. Establishing the construct validity of a violence risk assessment score presents a problem. How is the construct of risk defined? Should it be defined solely in terms of a history of violent actions or in terms of a constellation of individual and circumstantial factors? Research and theory reviewed in earlier chapters would suggest that the latter is the better approach. Although there is by no means perfect agreement on the factors associated with a propensity for committing a violent act, the range of factors are well established and do form a relatively coherent definition of risk for violent behavior.

The ability to evaluate construct validity also depends on the way in which the risk score is formed. It is difficult to establish the construct validity of risk assessments based on purely clinical judgments. The basis for the assessment is entirely subjective and difficult to access. On the other hand, risk assessments derived from standardized measures such as the broad-based risk/needs assessment forms can be more easily evaluated in terms of construct validity because the bases for the assessment are specified. For example, the variables

6
chapter

BEST PRACTICE
Evaluate the construct validity of a risk score in order to explain the basis for the assessment.

forming the basis for YLS/CMI risk assessments are identified and defined within the instrument. These constitute the construct of risk being assessed.

Additional procedures for evaluating construct validity involve comparing scores from a measure with scores from an alternative measure of the construct. This form of validity has been evaluated for most of the broad-based risk/needs instruments discussed in chapter 5. For example, scores from the YLS/CMI have been correlated significantly with scores from the SAVRY.

The construct validity of violence risk assessments should be of paramount concern in interpreting the assessments. It is not sufficient to simply categorize the youth as high or moderate risk or indicate that he has a high probability of committing a violent act. The basis for the assessment has to be made explicit. This information will be required by the court and should be made available to the client. The task of explaining the basis for the assessment is made easier where construct validity information is available. This issue will be discussed further in chapter 7.

Criterion-Related Predictive Validity

Criterion-related predictive validity is the second form of validity of particular relevance to assessments of risk for violent offending. The issue in this case concerns the ability of scores from the risk measure to actually predict future violent actions.

Evaluations of predictive validity are usually based on correlations between predictor and criterion variables. For example, the criterion-related validity of a personality test might be expressed as follows: $r = .66, p < .05$. The correlation value of .66 provides us with information about the strength of the association between test scores and the criterion, and the confidence index tells us that there are fewer than 5 chances in 100 of obtaining an association of that magnitude under chance circumstances (given a particular number of observations).

There are circumstances within forensic assessments, though, where more direct information about the predictive

Table 6.1 | Illustrations of Prediction Accuracy Contingency Tables

Part A: Illustration of terminology		
	Actual outcome	
	Reoffending	No reoffending
Predict reoffending	True positive	False positive
Predict no reoffending	False negative	True negative

Part B: Hypothetical illustration of a prediction accuracy contingency table			
	Actual outcome		
	Reoffended	No reoffending	N
Predict reoffending	106	52	158
Predict no reoffending	64	121	185
N	170	173	343

value of scores from risk assessments is required. *Contingency tables* are often useful in these cases. Table 6.1 provides an illustration of a contingency table. Part A describes the structure of a dichotomous contingency table. Two types of correct decisions (hits) are identified: *true positives* (positive prediction and positive outcome) and *true negatives* (negative prediction and negative outcome). Two types of incorrect predictions (misses) are also recognized: *false positives* (predict positive outcome but obtain negative) and *false negatives* (predict negative outcome but obtain positive).

Part B of the table presents an example of the use of a contingency table based on hypothetical data. The illustration involves forming two groups based on scores from an assessment battery, a high-risk group that is predicted to reoffend and a low-risk group predicted not to offend. The criterion measure in this case is also a dichotomous variable reflecting whether or not the participants actually reoffended within a 2-year period.

6
chapter

The hypothetical data indicate that 170 of the youth were actually charged with new crimes within the follow-up period, and 173 presented no evidence of criminal activity. Sixty-six percent of the predictions were correct in this case. This is based on adding the number of true positives (106) and true negatives (121) and dividing by the total number of cases. Thirty-four percent of the case were misses; that is, they involved predicting reoffending where none occurred (false positives) and predicting no offending where offending occurred (false negatives). Sixty-two percent of those who reoffended had been identified as high risk (106/170).

Analyzing contingency tables in this way can provide us with useful information about the predictive validity of our assessments, but interpreting the information is complicated by the fact that the values yielded are very sensitive to base rates and the cutoff used with the predictor (selection ratio). A variety of statistical solutions have been proposed for taking these factors into account in evaluating decision accuracy, including the Relative Improvement Over Chance, Receiver Operating Characteristics, and Common Language Effect Size Procedures (see Quinsey, Harris, Rice, & Cormier, 1998; Rice & Harris, 1995).

Considerable efforts have been made to evaluate at the adult level the predictive validity of actuarial and structured professional judgment assessments of propensity for violence (e.g., Bonta, Law, & Hanson, 1998; Heilbrun, in press). Reviews and meta-analyses of this research literature have concluded that both actuarial and structured professional judgment assessments are capable of yielding valid predictions of violent actions. Further, and as discussed earlier, these assessments are generally superior to unstructured clinical assessments. However, evidence supporting the predictive validity of the actuarial and structured professional judgment assessments is based on a relatively small sample of studies, and all of the reviewers conclude that additional research is needed on these methods as applied to the assessment of risk for violence on the part of adults.

Less research has been reported on the predictive validity of violence risk predictions yielded by assessments conducted with juveniles. Meta-analyses of the research that has been conducted (Edens et al., 2007; Schwalbe, 2007, 2008) have concluded that actuarial and structured professional judgment instruments are capable of yielding significant levels of validity in the prediction of reoffending in youth. The levels of predictive validity are comparable to those observed with the adult assessment tools. These reviewers also comment that validation research with the risk instruments has been based on a limited number of studies with a limited range of samples.

It must be kept in mind that most predictive validity information on an assessment measure will be limited to a particular time interval and particular situations. For example, some validation studies are based on the collection of reoffending data for a 2-year period following termination of the disposition. This provides only limited information regarding longer-term predictions. Also, most validation research is based on measuring reoffending within a community setting and may tell us little about the probability of reoffending in an institutional setting. The generalizability of validation results is a cause for concern.

Case Management Interpretation

Earlier discussions have stressed that two tasks are involved where a professional is asked to provide a violence risk assessment. The first involves the formation of an estimate of the likelihood the youth will engage in a violent act in the future and the second involves the identification of need factors that can assist in managing the risk.

Need Factors

Most of the broad-based risk/needs assessment tools discussed in chapter 4 have provided procedures for identifying needs associated with violence risk. These are simply the dynamic risk factors—the ones that can be changed, and, that if changed, reduce the probability that the youth will engage in future violent acts. However, the needs assessment component has been less researched and less standardized. Of particular value would be research linking the identification of need factors with case management plans and this in turn with

changes in risk levels. However, virtually no research of this type has yet been conducted.

Responsivity and Protective Factors

Case management also requires information about responsivity and protective factors. These are very important in developing case plans. Some standardized aptitude, personality, and behavioral measures are capable of providing information about responsivity factors. For example, the scores from an aptitude test such as the WISC-4 can assist in evaluating the youth's cognitive capacities that can, in turn, help determine the utility of interventions requiring a certain level of comprehension. Similarly, a measure such as the *Adolescent Psychopathology Scale* can help to identify pathological conditions that might interfere with certain therapeutic interventions. Some of the broad-based risk assessment instruments also provide for the collection information that can be interpreted to identify both responsivity and protective factors.

Identifying the Nature of the Threat

The focus of the discussion thus far in this volume has been on assessing a youth's propensity for engaging in a violent act and developing management strategies for reducing that threat. However, an estimate of the probability of committing a violent act depends not only on the characteristics of the youth but also on the circumstances under which the act is likely to occur. This dimension is generally not recognized in most violence risk assessments. The estimates generally reflect the likelihood of a violent act, and any effort to specify the probability of violence for a particular situation depends on a clinical judgment. This means that it is often important to collect information about the history of violent actions in specific situations as part of the risk assessment.

The terms threat assessment and targeted violence are often used to describe the situation where an estimate of the likelihood of violence in a particular situation is required. This situation is often

Table 6.2 | Steps in Combating School Violence

1. Do not ignore threats
2. Include clear written statements regarding threat management procedures.
3. Inform school staff, students, and parents about the procedures.
4. Appoint a school threat assessment coordinator.
5. Form a multidisciplinary threat management team.
6. Conduct full assessment of student presenting the threat.
7. Educate staff and students regarding cues to threatening individuals and situations.
8. Provide treatment to the student presenting the threat.
Note: *Threat Assessment in Schools: A Guide to Managing Threatening Situations and to Creating Safe School Climates*, R. A. Fein, B. Vossekuil, W. Pollack, R. Borum, W. Modzeleski, & M. Reddy, 2002, Washington, DC: U.S. Secret Service and U.S. Department of Education; *Assessment of Children: Behavioral, Social, and Clinical Foundations* (5th ed.), by J. M. Sattler & R. D. Hoge, 2006, San Diego, CA: Sattler Publishing Company.

encountered in institutional or school settings where there may be concerns about the likelihood of an act of violence. Though somewhat outside the scope of this volume, note should be made that procedures have been developed for assessing and managing situation-specific threats of violence (Borum et al., 1999; Fein & Vossekuil, 1998; Fein et al., 2002). Table 6.2 outlines key steps in such programs. It can be seen that estimating the youth's propensity for violence constitutes a key step in the process.

The Issue of Professional Overrides

Estimates of a youth's propensity for violence from clinical and structured professional judgment assessments depend ultimately on the judgment of the examiner. She evaluates and weighs the available information and subjectively forms an estimate of risk. The situation is somewhat different in the case of actuarial assessments where the risk estimate is based on a formula or algorithm. Although subjective judgments may be involved in entering information into the formula, there is no subjectivity in the final estimate. The question is whether there are circumstances under which the actuarial estimate can or should be overridden. Very limited research has been conducted on this issue (Heilbrun, in press), but it is not a critical issue in the case of juvenile violence risk assessments because true actuarial assessments are rarely involved.

Exercising Caution in Interpretation

Professionals conducting violence risks and needs assessments should be continually sensitive to the limits of their tools and methods. Although the use of standardized procedures, whether through actuarial or structured professional judgment approaches, can represent significant advances over clinical approaches, the professional should be aware of the limitations of those methods as well. The various precautions to be taken have been discussed at several points in this and previous chapters. The violence risk and need assessments are used to make important decisions about the youth, including pretrial detention, referrals to the mental health system, eligibility for alternative measures, and the kinds of post-adjudication dispositions and treatments provided. It is the responsibility of the professional conducting the assessment to be aware of the importance of the decisions and to use the assessments in a judicious manner.

Report Writing and Testimony | 7

T his chapter offers guidelines regarding the preparation of reports for forensic decisions and testimony in judicial settings. Guides for the preparation of reports will be available in some cases, and in other cases the professional has considerable latitude in the structure and content of a report. Similarly, statutory guidelines are sometimes available to guide expert testimony, including that of mental health professionals, and in other cases more latitude is available.

Reports focusing narrowly on an estimate of risk for violence or an evaluation of needs underlying the risk may be appropriate under some circumstances. In many cases, however, the violence risks and needs assessments constitute one part of the report with a larger focus. For example, an estimate of risk for violence may be included in a report relating to competency to stand trial, but it will be embedded in a larger assessment context. This chapter provides a discussion of some general and specific guidelines that will assist in the preparation of reports relating to violence risk and management decisions, followed by considerations regarding the presentation of judicial testimony.

Report Preparation

The structure and content of a report prepared to assist in a forensic decision will depend on the purpose of the report and the audience. A report designed to assist a judge or prosecuting attorney in making a postcharge detention decision will differ from one designed to assist a judge in determining an appropriate postadjudication disposition. The recommendations provided in this section follow the

BEWARE
Short reports
offer little information
about the basis
for risk assessment or needs
to be considered
in case management.

discussions of Heilbrun (2001), Heilbrun (in press), Heilbrun, Rogers, and Otto (2002), and Sattler and Hoge (2006).

Format of the Report

The length and format of the report will depend on the purpose and audience for the report.

SHORT REPORTS

For some purposes a short report focusing narrowly on risk for committing a violent act may be required, as, for example, in decisions regarding pretrial detention. These reports might be based solely on the completion of a checklist or brief interview with the youth. Short reports based on checklists of static risk factors are sometimes used in disposition and placement decisions as well. An example of one such instrument was presented in chapter 3.

Though these short reports may be economical to produce, they are seriously limited in some important respects (Heilbrun, in press). The brevity of the report means that little information is provided regarding the basis for the risk assessment. Further, the reports generally focus on static factors and provide little information about needs. In other words, they are of little value in case planning and management.

COMPREHENSIVE REPORTS

Comprehensive psychological or psychiatric reports will often be required in the case of decisions regarding competence to stand trial or postadjudication referrals for mental health treatment. These may be in a narrative or sectioned report form. Narrative reports are generally based on interview and file information and simply represent a written summary of the examiner's results and conclusions. The organization of the narrative report will be idiosyncratic to the examiner. Three potential problems can be noted regarding these reports. First, they are often based on purely clinical tools and do not represent the value associated with the use of more standardized assessment tools. Second, because the organization is idiosyncratic, reading these reports is more difficult than reading those with a higher level of organization. Finally, the language or terminology employed will vary among assessors, and this can contribute to confusion and misunderstanding.

Sectioned reports are organized under headings and subheadings to aid the reader. Most forensic mental health reports provided by psychologists and psychiatrists follow this type of format, although the actual organization of the report might differ.

INFO

Normally forensic mental health reports are organized around the following headings:

- Reason for the referral
- Sources of information
- Social background
- Criminal history
- Clinical impressions
- Assessment results
- Summary
- Recommendations

A case illustrating this type of format will be presented later in the chapter.

Sectioned reports are sometimes prepared by non-mental-health professionals as well. This would be illustrated by a probation officer preparing a predisposition report for the judge and basing the report on one of the broad-based risk/needs assessment tools described in chapter 4.

Sectioned reports are sometimes based on one of the broad-based risk/needs instruments described in chapter 4. The instruments help to guide the organization and language of the report. This introduces some consistency across reports to aid communication among professionals.

Even in the case of narrative and sectioned reports conciseness should be a paramount goal. It is important to identify and evaluate all of the information utilized in the assessment and to discuss the reasoning behind the conclusions. However, this should be done in as concise a manner as possible, with a careful focus on the purpose of the report.

BEST PRACTICE

Strive for conciseness even when writing a comprehensive report.

Content of the Report

The content of the report will be determined by its purpose. If the need is simply for

an estimate of risk for the likelihood of commission of a violent act, then the report would contain a statement of the estimate and an explanation of the basis for the estimate. The latter is important from the point of view of explaining (and defending) the estimate to judges or attorneys and, as was discussed earlier, important from an ethical point of view. Professionals should not provide judgments of individuals without providing justifications for the judgments.

An expanded content in the report will be required where information about risks and needs is needed for case planning and management decisions. Here the report should provide sufficient information to identify specific needs related to the violence risk and, where appropriate, recommendations for addressing the risk factors. This type of report would be required, for example, where a prosecuting attorney is deciding whether the youth would be eligible for a pretrial diversion program and, if eligible, the kinds of treatment that would be appropriate in that program.

Wherever recommendations relating to case planning and management are to be developed, it is important to elaborate the bases for the risks and needs assessment. It is not sufficient to say that the youth is at overall moderate risk for reoffending, with high levels of risk shown on family circumstances/parenting and antisocial peer associations. The nature of those areas of risk and need should be fully elaborated.

An important practical issue that arises in this context concerns the kind of information that would not be appropriate in a forensic report. Two general rules apply in this case. First, information that is not relevant to the purpose of the report should not be included. If, for example, the only purpose of the report is to estimate a youth's risk for an immediate violent act, then information about family background may not be considered relevant.

A second and related rule is that particular care should be taken not to include information beyond the purpose of the report that may be prejudicial to the youth and violate rules of due process

(Melton, Petrila, Poythress, & Slobogin, 2007). This situation might arise where an estimate of risk for violence emerges as part of a forensic assessment but where such an estimate is not relevant to the forensic decision being addressed.

BEWARE
Do not include irrelevant or prejudicial information in the report.

Reporting Scores and Diagnoses

RISK ASSESSMENT

Appropriate terminology to be used in reporting risk assessments is an issue that frequently arises. The issue is straightforward in the case of actuarial measures yielding mechanically derived risk categories or probabilities of reoffending. The Level of Service Inventory-Revised (LSI-R) developed for adult offenders provides an example. This measure expresses scores in terms of three levels of risk (low, moderate, high) and probabilities of reoffending (e.g., a raw score of 31 corresponds to a 68% probability of reoffending based on the incidence of reoffending in a sample of adult male offenders). These are empirically derived estimates. The meaning of this type of score is generally clear to nonprofessionals, although it is important to explain the basis for the scoring and the cautions associated with their interpretation when using the scores.

Risk assessment tools for juveniles do not employ absolute estimates of the probability of reoffending. However, two of the broad-based instruments described earlier, the YLS/CMI and WSJCA, provide actuarial scores reflecting levels of risk (low, moderate, high, and very high in the former case). The structured professional judgment instruments described in chapter 4 also provide for expressing level of risk in terms of discrete categories.

One of the structured professional judgment instruments, the SAVRY, provides for estimating the level of risk in terms of three categories: low, moderate, and high. It also provides some additional guidelines for reporting judgments of risk and need based on the measure (Boer, Hart, Kripp, & Webster, 1997):

- Report level of risk for a violent act if no efforts are made to address identified needs.
- Estimate probable nature of future violence.

7
chapter

- Identify the likely victim of any future violence.
- Identify situations or contexts that might increase risk for violence.
- Identify steps that can be taken to reduce the risk of committing a violent act.

Information underlying these reports are based on professional judgments reached using the SAVRY assessment.

The larger issue of the ethics of communicating risk predictions has been addressed by Grisso and Appelbaum (1992), Heilbrun (in press), and Heilbrun, O'Neill, Strohman, Bowman, and Philipson (2000). Their conclusion is that communicating risk predictions for forensic decisions can be justified as long as the prediction rules are empirically supported, the prediction is relevant to the client's situation, and other ethical guidelines are followed. They also conclude that the predictions of risk should be expressed in categorical (e.g., low, moderate, or high level of risk) or frequency terms (e.g., 30 individuals with this score reoffended within 2 years).

STANDARDIZED TESTS

Issues concerning the reporting of scores from standardized tests may also arise. Personality and cognitive aptitude tests are sometimes used as part of comprehensive assessments. They may contribute to the risks and needs assessment and provide information regarding responsivity or protective factors.

It is appropriate to report scores from measures where the scores are easy to interpret and relate clearly to the purpose of the report. For example, scores from some of the rating/checklist measures can be reported in a straightforward manner:

> David obtained *T-scores* above 70 (93rd to 97th percentiles) on the Social Problems and Rule Breaking subscales of the Child Behavior Checklist Teacher Report form, placing him in the clinical range compared with a sample of youth in his age group.

This information is generally well understood by non-mental-health professionals.

However, other types of scores are more technical and may not be accessible to people unfamiliar with the interpretation of scores. For example, scores from the MMPI-A are expressed as codetypes such as "codetype 4-6/6-4, with an elevation on A-ang." These are essentially meaning-

BEWARE
When reporting clinical diagnoses, point out that their relationship to risk of violence is not established.

less to someone unfamiliar with the scoring of this instrument. This score would have to be interpreted in layman's terms. One possible solution to this type of issue is to include all technical information in an appendix to the report. Another is to explain the meaning of this codetype in sufficient detail and nontechnical language to allow the reader to understand the interpretation if not the codetype.

CLINICAL DIAGNOSES

A special issue arises in the case of reporting clinical diagnoses in reports prepared by mental health professionals. Should a diagnosis such as conduct disorder, antisocial personality disorder, or bipolar disorder be used in a violence risk assessment? The argument against including such statements is that the link between the diagnostic disorders and violence is not always clear and is sometimes misunderstood (Heilbrun, in press; Melton et al., 2007). Often, of course, the violence risk assessment is contained in a broader report where the diagnosis may be relevant. In this case, however, it must be made clear that the diagnosis may not directly inform the risk assessment.

Clarity of Language

Recommendations regarding the reporting of scores relate to a larger issue, which concern the nature of the language used in the report:

> You want the reader to comprehend your report with a minimum of effort. Check carefully that you have written an understandable report, and revise any potentially confusing sentences. You will enhance communication if you write concisely, follow rules of grammar and punctuation, use a consistent style, make clear transitions between different ideas or topics, and give examples of the examinee's performance. Technical and professional writing should leave little room for misinterpretation. Because your report

BEWARE
Be cautious in
how you report
informal observations
of the youth.

will likely be read by several people
who have different levels of
psychological knowledge, write it in a
way that will be clear to all readers.
(Sattler & Hoge, 2006, p. 598)

These recommendations are particularly important in the case of forensic assessments where reports may be read by judges, prosecuting and defense attorneys, correctional officers, and others unfamiliar with the language of psychological assessment.

Use of Observations

Unless the report is based exclusively on the use of static variables in an actuarial index of the likelihood of committing a violent offense, informal observations of the client's behavior during the assessment are relevant and may be included in the report. These observations will certainly be employed in unstructured clinical assessments, but they may also be used in structured professional judgment assessments. Observations collected during the interview may be involved in responding to items within the procedure. For example, the item "attention problems" appears in some of the broad-based risk/ needs assessments. The assessor's response to this item will depend on information revealed in the interview or other sources of information, but it could also be informed by observations made in the course of interacting with the youth. Observations can also be used to supplement and elaborate the summary risk assessments.

However, caution should be observed in reporting informal observations. The distinction between describing and interpreting a behavior must be kept in mind. It is one thing to report that the youth spent time staring out the window and often asked to have questions repeated, and another to conclude that the youth has an attentional disorder. It is also important to remember that behaviors observed during the assessment sessions may not generalize to other situations.

Integrating and Reconciling Information

Information collected from different sources often conflict with one another. For example, a parent may report that the youth

Table 7.1 | Knowledge Areas Essential for Effective Forensic Testimony

- Understand the effects of forensic settings on the assessment process.

- Understand the functioning of applicable administrative, correctional, and court systems.

- Understand the statutory administrative or case law of the specific legal context where assessment occurs.

- Understand how to communicate with attorneys and judges.

- Understand how to give testimony in a deposition or in court.

Note: From "APA's Guidelines for Test User Qualifications," by S. M. Turner, S. T. DeMers, H. R. Fox, and G. M. Reed, 2001, *American Psychologist, 56*, pp. 1099–1113.

is highly aggressive and confrontational, whereas a teacher's report and the results from a personality test may indicate no problems in this respect. In some cases the contradictions arise from variations in behavior across settings, and in other cases one or the other source of information may simply be unreliable. The question of reliability is, of course, a particular problem with information collected in an interview with the youth.

There is no simple solution to this issue. The assessor must report the conflict in the report and use his professional judgment to resolve the contradictions to the extent possible. Certainly the presence of conflicting information from different sources is a basis for exercising caution in reaching conclusions.

A particular problem arises in evaluating information from alternative sources regarding the likelihood the youth will engage in a violent action. There is such a fear of false negatives that a tendency exists to overestimate the probability of such an

BEST PRACTICE

Report information from all sources and use your judgment to reconcile conflicts to the extent possible.

action. This is certainly observed in school settings where prominent incidents of school shootings have created a nervous environment where teachers and principals sometimes mislabel youth as violence prone. The use of standardized assessment tools will help to provide a guard against this type of distorting information, but ultimately it comes down to the judgment of the assessor.

Offering Expert Testimony

Although relatively rare, mental health professionals may occasionally be called to testify in a court or other judicial tribunal as expert witnesses. Other professionals conducting violence risks and needs assessments may also be required to testify. For example, probation officers are often asked to offer guidance to judges in determining dispositions, and these may involve estimates of the likelihood of engaging in a violent action.

It is important to take the testimony process seriously. The performance of the professional will affect not only her reputation, but that of the profession as well. A variety of factors affect the quality of the testimony:

> Your effectiveness as an expert witness will be judged on whether you considered all of the relevant facts, whether the judge and jury are confident about the accuracy of the facts underlying your opinion, whether you showed an adequate understanding of the pertinent clinical and scientific principles involved in the case, whether you used methods of assessment and analysis recognized as appropriate by professionals in your field, whether the inferences you drew were logical, whether your assumptions were reasonable, and whether you were reasonably objective. Therefore, you want your testimony to be thorough, clear, logical, consistent, explainable, and objective. (Sattler & Hoge, 2006; p. 75)

Guidance regarding the testimony process has been offered by Barsky and Gould (2002), Heilbrun (2001), and Sattler and Hoge (2006).

Qualifications as an Expert

It is important to establish credentials for offering expert testimony when someone is testifying as a mental health professional or as any other professional such as a probation officer or a social worker. Educational and professional experience are important in this respect. Clinical certification as a psychologist or psychiatrist is probably essential in the case of these professions, and possessing Diplomate status with the American Board of Forensic Psychology is desirable. These certification processes help to guarantee that the minimal professional standards are met in training programs and that the professional's performance is monitored.

BEWARE
Counsel may cross-examine on the basis of the written assessment report.

Expertise in the mental health area that forms the focus of the testimony is essential, but expertise relating to the judicial process is also important. Turner, DeMers, Fox, and Reed (2001) have identified the specific areas of knowledge essential for effective forensic testimony (see Table 7.1). A full understanding of the relevant ethical and legal principles is essential.

Quality of the Assessment Report

The success of the expert testimony will depend directly on the quality of the assessment report. The expert witness will base his verbal testimony on the information provided in the report. The court or counsel may also review the written report. Assessors preparing incomplete, biased, or misleading reports will often be challenged by counsel.

Presentation Style

Heilbrun (2001) has shown that stylistic effectiveness is critical to the effectiveness of an expert's testimony. Style of dress and familiarity with courtroom procedures and etiquette are essential to making an effective presentation. The ability to communicate clearly to judges, counsel, and jury members is also important.

Final Words

This volume has addressed a variety of issues relating to the conduct and reporting of forensic assessments of juveniles, with particular

7
chapter

attention to assessing violence risk and management. The importance of adhering to national and local legal guidelines and policies has been stressed, as has the necessity for observing the ethical principles governing the assessor's profession.

The reports are generally prepared for courts or other judicial bodies to assist in legal decisions. As such, the assessor will be bound by the rules and policies governing those decisions. However, it must be kept in mind that the subject of these assessments are young people, and there is also an obligation to endeavor to address the needs of youth and assist them to develop into law-abiding and productive citizens. The benefits of this goal for society are very great.

References

Achenbach, T. M. (1995). Diagnosis, assessment, and comorbidity in psychosocial treatment research. *Journal of Abnormal Child Psychology, 23*, 45–66.

Achenbach, T. M. (1999). The Child Behavior Checklist and related instruments. In M. E. Maruish (Ed.), *The use of psychological testing for treatment planning and outcomes assessment* (2nd ed., pp. 429–466). Mahwah, NJ: Lawrence Erlbaum Associates.

Altschuler, D. M. (1998). Intermediate sanctions and community treatment for serious and violent offenders. In R. Loeber & D. P. Farrington (Eds.), *Serious and violent juvenile offenders: Risk factors and successful interventions* (pp. 367–385). Thousand Oaks, CA: Sage.

American Academy of Psychiatry and the Law. (1995). *Ethical guidelines for the practice of forensic psychiatry*. Bloomfield, CT: Author.

American Educational Research Association, American Psychological Association, National Council on Education. (1999). *Standards for educational and psychological testing*. Washington, DC: Author.

American Psychiatric Association. (2000). *Diagnostic and statistical manual of mental disorders: Text revision (DSM-IV-TR)*. Washington, DC: Author.

American Psychological Association. (1988). *Code of fair testing practices in education*. Washington, DC: Author.

American Psychological Association. (1986). *Guidelines for computer-based tests and interpretations*. Washington, DC: Author.

American Psychological Association. (1990). *Guidelines for providers of psychological services to ethnic, linguistic, and culturally diverse populations*. Washington, DC: Author.

Andrews, D. A., & Bonta, J. (2006). *The psychology of criminal conduct* (4th ed.). Cincinnati, OH: Anderson.

Andrews, D. A., Bonta, J., & Hoge, R. D. (1990). Classification for effective rehabilitation: Rediscovering psychology. *Criminal Justice and Behavior, 17*, 19–52.

Andrews, D. A., & Dowden, C. (2005). Managing correctional treatment for reduced recidivism: A meta-analytic review of program integrity. *Legal and Criminological Psychology, 10*, 173–187.

Archer, R. P., Bolinskey, P. K., Morton, T. L., & Farris, K. L. (2003). MMPI-A characteristics of male adolescents in juvenile justice and clinical treatment settings. *Assessment, 10*, 400–410.

Arseneault, L., Tremblay, R. E., Boulerice, B., & Saucier, J. F. (2002). Obstetric complications and adolescent violent behaviors: Testing two developmental pathways. *Child Development, 73*, 496–508.

Barbaree, H. E., & Marshall, W. L. (Eds.). (2006). *The juvenile sex offender* (2nd ed.). New York: Guilford.

Barkan, S. E. (2006). *Criminology: A sociological understanding.* Upper Saddle River, NJ: Pearson Prentice-Hall.

Barnoski, R., & Markussen, S. (2005). Washington State Juvenile Court Assessment. In T. Grisso, G. Vincent, & D. Seagrave (Eds.), *Mental health screening and assessment in juvenile justice* (pp. 271–282). New York: Guilford.

Barsky, A. E., & Gould, J. W. (2002). *Clinicians in court: A guide to subpoenas, depositions, testifying, and everything else you need to know.* New York: Guilford.

Bersoff, D. N. (1995). *Ethical conflicts in psychology.* Washington, DC: American Psychological Association.

Bird, H. R., Yager, T. J., Staghezza, B., Gould, M. S., Canino, G., & Rubio-Stipec, M. (1990). Impairment in the epidemiological measurement of childhood psychopathology in the community. *Journal of the American Academy of Child and Adolescent Psychiatry, 29*, 796–803.

Blumstein, A., Farrington, D. P., & Moitra, S. D. (1985). Delinquency careers: Innocents, desisters, and persisters. In M. Tonry & N. Morris (Eds.), *Crime and justice: An annual review of research* (pp. 137–168). Chicago, IL: University of Chicago Press.

Boer, D. P., Hart, S. D., Kropp, P. R., & Webstern C. D. (1997). *Manual for the Sexual Violence Risk–20.* Burnaby, British Columbia, Canada: Simon Fraser University, Mental Health, Law, and Policy Institute.

Bonta, J. S., Law, M, & Hanson, R. K. (1998). The prediction of criminal and violent recidivism among mentally disordered offenders: A meta-analysis. *Psychological Bulletin, 122*, 123–142.

Borum, R. (2006). Assessing risk for violence among juvenile offenders. In S. Sparta & G. Koocher (Eds.), *The forensic assessment of children and adolescents: Issues and applications* (pp. 190–202). New York: Oxford University Press.

Borum, R., Bartel, P. A., & Forth, A. E. (2005). Structured assessment of violence risk in youth. In T. Grisso, G. Vincent, & D. Seagrave (Eds.), *Mental health screening and assessment in juvenile justice* (pp. 311–323). New York: Guilford.

Borum, R., Fein, R., Vossekuil, B., & Berglund, J. (1999). Threat assessment: Defining an approach for evaluating risk of targeted violence. *Behavioral Sciences and the Law, 17*, 332–337.

Borum, R., & Verhaagen, D. (2006). *Assessing and managing violence risk in youth.* New York: Guilford.

Boxer, P., & Frick, P. J. (2008). Treatment of violent offenders. In R. D. Hoge, N. G. Guerra, & P. Boxer (Eds.), *Treating the juvenile offender* (pp. 147–170). New York: Guilford.

Bronfenbrenner, U. (1979). *The ecology of human development.* Cambridge, MA: Harvard University Press.

Bronfenbrenner, U. (1986). Ecology of the family as a context for human development: Research perspectives. *Developmental Psychology, 22,* 723–742.

Butcher, J. N., Williams, C. L., Graham, J. R., Archer, R. P., Tellegen, A., Ben-Porath, Y. S., et al. (1992). *Minnesota Multiphasic Personality Inventory—Adolescent.* Minneapolis, MN: University of Minnesota Press.

Caspi, A, McClay, J., Moffitt, T., Mill, J., Martin, J., Craig, I. W., et al. (2002). Role of genotype in the cycle of violence in maltreated children. *Science, 297,* 851–854.

Catalano, R. F., & Hawkins, J. D. (1996). The social development model: A theory of antisocial behavior. In J. D. Hawkins (Ed.), *Delinquency and crime: Current theories* (pp. 149–197). Cambridge, UK: Cambridge University Press.

Cauffman, E., & Steinberg, L. (2000). (Im)maturity of judgment in adolescence: Why adolescents may be less culpable than adults. *Behavioral Sciences and the Law, 18,* 1–21.

Cernkovich, S. A., Giordano, P. C., & Rudolph, J. L. (2000). Race, crime, and the American Dream. *Journal of Research in Crime and Delinquency, 37,* 131–170.

Cicchetti, D., & Cohen, D. (1995). *Developmental psychopathology.* New York: Wiley.

Cicchetti, D., & Rogosch, F. (2002). A developmental psychopathology perspective on adolescence. *Journal of Consulting and Clinical Psychology, 70,* 6–20.

Committee on Ethical Guidelines for Forensic Psychologists. (1991). Specialty guidelines for forensic psychologists. *Law and Human Behavior, 15,* 655–665.

Compas, B. E., Hinden, B. R., & Gerhardt, C. A. (1995). Adolescent development: Pathways and processes of risk and resilience. *Annual Review of Psychology, 46,* 265–293.

Corrado, R. R. (1992). Introduction. In R. R. Corrado, N. Bala, R. Linden, & M. Le Blanc (Eds.), *Juvenile justice in Canada: A theoretical and analytical assessment* (pp. 1–20). Toronto, ON: Buttersworth.

Dishion, T. J., McCord, J., & Poulin, F. (1999). When interventions harm: Peer groups and problem behavior. *American Psychologist, 54,* 755–764.

Dodge, K. A. (1986). A social information-processing model of science competence in children. In M. Perlmutter (Ed.), *Minnesota symposium in child psychology* (pp. 77–125). Hillsdale, NJ: Erlbaum.

Dodge, K. A. (2003). Do social information processing patterns mediate aggressive behavior? In B. B. Lahey, T. E. Moffitt, & A. Caspi (Eds.), *Causes of conduct disorder and juvenile delinquency* (pp. 254–274). New York: Guilford.

Dodge, K. A., Dishion, T. J., & Lansford, J. E. (Eds.). (2006). *Deviant peer influences in programs for youth: Problems and solutions.* New York: Guilford.

Dodge, K. A., & Rabiner, D. L. (2004). Returning to roots: Social information processing and moral development. *Child Development, 75*, 1003–1008.

Edens, J. F., Campbell, J. S., & Weir, J. M. (2007). Youth psychopathy and criminal recidivism: A meta-analysis of the psychopathy checklist measures. *Law and Human Behavior, 31*, 53–75.

Edens, J. F., Skeem, J., Cruise, K., & Cauffman, E. (2001). Assessment of "juvenile psychopathy" and its association with violence: A critical review. *Behavioral Sciences and the Law, 19*, 53–80.

Elliott, D. S., Hamburg, B., & Williams, K. R. (Eds.). (1998). *Violence in American Schools: A new perspective.* Cambridge, UK: Cambridge University Press.

Essau, C. A., Sasagawa, S., & Frick, P. J. (2006). Callous-unemotional traits in a community sample of adolescents. *Assessment, 13*, 454–469.

Eyde, L. D., Robertson, G. J., Krug, S. E., Moreland, K. C., Robertson, A. G., Shewan, C. M., et al. (1993). *Responsible test use: Case studies for assessing human behavior.* Washington, DC: American Psychological Association.

Farrington, D. P. (1994). Childhood, adolescent, and adult features of violent males. In L. R. Huesmann (Ed.), *Aggressive behavior: Current perspectives* (pp. 215–240). New York: Plenum.

Farrington, D. P. (1998). Predictors, causes and correlates of male youth violence. In M. Tonry & M. H. Moore (Eds.), *Youth violence (Crime and Justice, vol. 24)* (pp. 421–475). Chicago, IL: University of Chicago Press.

Farrington, D. P. (2003). Key results from the first 40 years of the Cambridge Study in Delinquent Development. In T. P. Thornberry & M. D. Krohn (Eds.), *Taking stock of delinquency: An overview of findings from contemporary longitudinal studies* (pp. 137–183). Boston, MA: Kluwer.

Farrington, D. P. (2004). Conduct disorder, aggression, and delinquency. In R. M. Lerner & L. Steinberg (Eds.), *Handbook of adolescent psychology* (2nd ed., pp. 627–624). New York: Wiley.

Farrington, D. P. (2006). Key longitudinal-experimental studies in criminology. *Journal of Experimental Criminology, 2*, 121–141.

Fein, R., & Vossekuil, B. (1998). *Protective intelligence and threat assessment investigations: A guide for state and local law enforcement officials* (NIJ/

OJP/DOJ Publications No. 170612). Washington, DC: U.S. Department of Justice.

Fein, R., Vossekuil, B., Pollack, W., Borum, R., Modzeleski, W., & Reddy, M. (2002). *Threat assessment in the schools: A guide to managing threatening situations and to creating safe school climates.* Washington, DC: U.S. Secret Service and U.S. Department of Education.

Feld, B. C. (1999). *Bad kids: Race and the transformation of the juvenile court.* New York: Oxford University Press.

Forth, A. E. (2005). Hare psychopathy checklist: Youth version. In T. Grisso, G. Vincent, & D. Seagrave (Eds.), *Mental health screening and assessment in juvenile justice* (pp. 324–338). New York: Guilford.

Frick, P. J. (2006). Developmental pathways to conduct disorder. *Child and Adolescent Psychiatric Clinics of North America, 15,* 311–332.

Garb, H. N. (2000). Computers will become increasingly important for psychological assessment: Not that there's anything wrong with that! *Assessment, 12,* 31–39.

Geisinger, K. F., Spies, R. A., Carlson, J. F., & Plake, B. S. (2007). *The seventeenth mental measurements yearbook.* Lincoln, NB: Buros Institute of Mental Measurement.

Gibbs, J. C., Barriga, A. Q., & Potter, G. B. (2001). *How I Think (HIT) questionnaire.* Champaign, IL: Research Press.

Gottfredson, M. R., & Hirschi, T. (1990). *A general theory of crime.* Stanford, CA: Stanford University Press.

Grisso, T. (1998). *Forensic evaluation of juveniles.* Sarasota, FL: Professional Resource Press.

Grisso, T. (2003). *Evaluating competencies: Forensic assessments and instruments* (2nd ed.). New York: Kluwer Academic/Plenum.

Grisso, T. (2004). *Double jeopardy: Adolescent offenders with mental disorders.* Chicago, IL: University of Chicago Press.

Grisso, T. (2005a). Why we need mental health screening and assessment in juvenile justice programs. In T. Grisso, G. Vincent, & D. Seagrave (Eds.), *Mental health screening and assessment in juvenile justice* (pp. 3–21). New York: Guilford.

Grisso, T. (2005b). Evaluating the properties of instruments for screening and assessment. In T. Grisso, G. Vincent, & D. Seagrave (Eds.), *Mental health screening and assessment in juvenile justice* (pp. 71–97). New York: Guilford.

Grisso, T., & Appelbaum, P. S. (1992). Is it unethical to offer predictions of future violence? *Law and Human Behavior, 16,* 621–633.

Grisso, T., & Appelbaum, P. S. (1998). *Assessing competence to consent to treatment: A guide for physicians and other health professionals.* Oxford, UK: Oxford University Press.

Grisso, T., & Schwartz, R. G. (Eds.). (2000). *Youth on trial: A developmental perspective on juvenile justice.* Chicago, IL: University of Chicago Press.

Grisso, T., & Vincent, G. (2005). The context for mental health screening and assessment. In T. Grisso, G. Vincent, & D. Seagrave (Eds.), *Mental health screening and assessment in juvenile justice* (pp. 44–70). New York: Guilford.

Grove, W. M., & Meehl, P. E. (1996). Comparative efficiency of informal (subjective, impressionistic) and formal (mechanical, algorithmic) prediction procedures: The clinical–statistical controversy. *Psychology, Public Policy, and the Law, 2,* 293–323.

Grove, W. M., Zald, D. H., Lebow, B. S., Snitz, B. E., & Nelson, C. (2000). Clinical versus mechanical prediction: A meta-analysis. *Psychological Assessment, 12,* 19–30.

Guerra, N. G., Williams, K. R., Tolan, P. H., & Modecki, K. L. (2008a). Theoretical and research advances in understanding the causes of juvenile offending. In R. D. Hoge, N. G. Guerra, & P. Boxer (Eds.), *Treating the juvenile offender* (pp. 33–53). New York: Guilford.

Guerra, N. G., Kim, T. E., & Boxer, P. (2008b). What works: Best practices with juvenile offenders. In R. D. Hoge, N. G. Guerra, & P. Boxer (Eds.), *Treating the juvenile offender* (pp. 79–102). New York: Guilford.

Hare, R. D. (1998). The Hare PCL-R: Some issues concerning its use and misuse. *Legal and Criminological Psychology, 3,* 99–119.

Hare, R. D. (2003). *The Hare Psychopathy Checklist–Revised* (2nd ed.). Toronto, ON: Multi-Health Systems.

Hawkins, J. D., Herrenkohl, T., Farrington, D. P., Brewer, D., Catalano, R. F., & Harachi, T. W. (1998). A review of predictors of youth violence. In R. Loeber & D. P. Farrington (Eds.), *Serious and violent juvenile offenders: Risk factors and successful interventions* (pp. 106–146). Thousand Oaks, CA: Sage.

Heilbrun, K. (1997). Prediction vs. management models relevant to risk assessment: The importance of legal decision-making context. *Law and Human Behavior, 21,* 347–359.

Heilbrun, K. (2001). *Principles of forensic mental health assessment.* New York: Kluwer Academic/Plenum.

Heilbrun, K. (in press). *Violence risk assessment in adults.* New York: Oxford University Press.

Heilbrun, K., Lee, R., & Cottle, C. (2005). Risk factors and intervention outcomes: Meta-analyses of juvenile offending. In K. Heilbrun, N. Goldstein, & R. Redding (Eds.), *Juvenile delinquency: Prevention, assessment and interventions* (pp. 111–133). New York: Oxford University Press.

Heilbrun, K., O'Neill, M., Strohman, L. Bowman, Q., & Philipson, J. (2000). Expert approaches to communicating violence risk. *Law and Human Behavior, 24*, 137–148.

Heilbrun, K., Rogers, R., & Otto, R. (2002). Forensic assessment: Current status and future directions. In J. Ogloff (Ed.), *Psychology and law: Reviewing the discipline* (pp. 120–147). New York: Kluwer Academic/Plenum Press.

Hoge, R. D. (in press). Developmental perspectives on offending. In J. Brown & E. Campbell (Eds.), *The Cambridge Handbook of Forensic Psychology*. Cambridge, UK: Cambridge University Press.

Hoge, R. D. (1999a). An expanded role for psychological assessments in juvenile justice systems. *Criminal Justice and Behavior, 26*, 251–266.

Hoge, R. D. (1999b). *Assessing adolescents in educational, counseling, and other settings*. Mahwah, NJ: Earlbaum.

Hoge, R. D. (2001). *The juvenile offender: Theory, research, and applications*. Norwell, MA: Kluwer.

Hoge, R. D. (2008). Assessment in juvenile justice systems. In R. D. Hoge, N. G. Guerra, & P. Boxer (Eds.), *Treating the juvenile offender* (pp. 54–75). New York: Guilford.

Hoge, R. D., & Andrews, D. A. (1996). *Assessing the youthful offender: Issues and techniques*. New York: Plenum.

Jessor, R. (1992). Risk behavior in adolescence: A psychosocial framework for understanding and action. In D. E. Rogers & E. Ginsberg (Eds.), *Adolescents at risk: Mental and social perspectives* (pp. 19–34). Boulder, CO: Westview.

Kohlberg, L. (1984). *The psychology of moral development*. New York: Harper & Rowe.

Krisberg, B., & Howell, J. C. (1998). The impact of the juvenile justice system and prospects for graduated sanctions in a comprehensive strategy. In R. Loeber & D. P. Farrington (Eds.), *Serious and violent juvenile offenders: Risk factors and successful interventions* (pp. 346–366). Thousand Oaks, CA: Sage.

Krisberg, B., Hartney, C., Wolf, A., & Silva, F. (2009). *Youth violence myths and realities: A tale of three cities*. Washington, DC: National Council on Crime and Delinquency.

Kruh, I. P., Frick, P. J., & Clements, C. B. (2005). Historical and personality correlates of the violence patterns of juveniles tried as adults. *Criminal Justice and Behavior, 32*, 69–96.

Le Blanc, M. (1998). Screening of serious and violent juvenile offenders: Identification, classification, and prediction. In R. Loeber & D. P. Farrington (Eds.), *Serious and violent juvenile offenders: Risk factors and successful interventions* (pp. 167–193). Thousand Oaks, CA: Sage.

Lerner, R. M. (1991). Changing organism-context relations as the basic process of development: A developmental-contextual perspective. *Developmental Psychology, 27*, 27–32.

Lerner, R. M. (1995). *America's youth in crisis: Challenges and options for programs and policies.* Thousand Oaks, CA: Sage.

Lipsey, M. W. (1995). What do we learn from 400 research studies on the effectiveness of treatment with juvenile delinquents? In. J. McGuire (Ed.), *What works: Reducing reoffending* (pp. 63–78). Chistester, UK: Wiley.

Lipsey, M. W. (2006). The effects of community-based group treatment for delinquency. In K. A. Dodge, T. J. Dishion, & J. E. Lansford (Eds.), *Deviant peer influences in programs for youth: Problems and solutions* (pp. 162–184). New York: Guilford.

Lipsey, M. W., & Derzon, J. H. (1998). Predictors of violent or serious delinquency in adolescence and early adulthood: A synthesis of longitudinal research. In R. Loeber & D. P. Farrington (Eds.), *Serious and violent juvenile offenders: Risk factors and successful interventions* (pp. 86–105). Thousand Oaks, CA: Sage.

Lipsey, M. W., & Wilson, D. B. (1998). Effective intervention for serious juvenile offenders: A synthesis of research. In R. Loeber & D. P. Farrington (Eds.), *Serious and violent juvenile offenders: Risk factors and successful interventions* (pp. 313–345). Thousand Oaks, CA: Sage.

Loeber, R. (1988). Natural histories of conduct problems, delinquency, and associated substance use: Evidence for developmental progressions. In B. B. Lahey & A. E. Kazdin (Eds.), *Advances in clinical psychology* (Vol. 11, pp. 73–125). New York: Plenum.

Loeber, R., & Farrington, D. P. (Eds.). (1998). *Serious and violent juvenile offenders: Risk factors and successful interventions.* Thousand Oaks, CA: Sage.

Loeber, R., & Farrington, D. P. (2000). Young children who commit crimes: Epidemiology, developmental origins, risk factors, early interventions, and policy implications. *Development and Psychopathology, 12*, 737–762.

Loeber, R., Farrington, D. P., & Waschbusch, D. A. (1998). Serious and violent juvenile offenders. In R. Loeber & D. P. Farrington (Eds.), *Serious and violent juvenile offenders: Risk factors and successful interventions* (pp. 13–29). Thousand Oaks, CA: Sage.

Maguire, K., & Pastore, A. L. (Eds.) (1995). *Sourcebook of criminal justice statistics.* Washington, DC: Government Printing Office.

Maguire, K., & Pastore, A. L. (1996). *Bureau of Justice Statistics sourcebook of criminal justice statistics, 1995.* Albany, NY: The Hindelang Criminal Justice Research Center, State University of New York at Albany.

Mannheim, H. (1965). *Comparative criminology*. Boston, MA: Houghton Mifflin.

Matarazzo, J. D. (1992). Psychological testing and assessment in the 21st century. *American Psychologist, 47*, 1007–1018.

Melton, G., Petrila, J., Poythress, N. G., & Slobogin, C. (2007). *Psychological evaluations for the courts: A handbook for mental health professionals and lawyers* (2nd ed.). New York: Guilford.

Messick, S. (1995). Validity of psychological assessment: Validation of inferences from persons' responses and performances as scientific inquiry into score meaning. *American Psychologist, 50*, 741–749.

Miller, W. R., & Rollnick, S. (2002). *Motivational interviewing* (2nd ed.). New York: Guilford.

Millon, T. (1993). *Millon Adolescent Clinical Inventory*. Minneapolis, MN: National Computer Systems.

Moffitt, T. E. (2003). Life-course-persistent and adolescence-limited antisocial behavior: A 10-year research review and research agenda. In B. B. Lahey, T. E. Moffitt, & A. Caspi (Eds.), *Causes of conduct disorder and juvenile delinquency* (pp. 49–75). New York: Guilford.

Moffitt, T. E. (2006). Life-course-persistent versus adolescence-limited antisocial behavior. In D. Cicchetti & D. Cohen (Eds.), *Developmental Psychopathology* (2nd ed., pp. 570–598). New York: Wiley.

Moffitt, T. E., Caspi, A., Rutter, M., & Silva, P. A. (2001). *Sex differences in antisocial behaviour: Conduct disorder, delinquency, and violence in the Dunedin Longitudinal Study*. Cambridge, UK: Cambridge University Press.

Morgan, A. B., & Lilienfeld, S. O. (2000). A meta-analytic review of the relation between antisocial behavior and neuropsychological and neuropsychological measures of executive function. *Clinical Psychology Review, 20*, 113–136.

Nagin, D. S., & Tremblay, R. E. (1999). Trajectories of boys' physical aggression, opposition, and hyperactivity on the path to physically violent and non-violent juvenile delinquency. *Child Development, 70*, 1181–1196.

Nathan, P. E., & Langenbucher, J. W. (1999). Psychopathology: Description and classification. *Annual Review of Psychology, 50*, 79–107.

National Center for Education Statistics. (2006). *The pocket condition of education 2006*. Washington, DC: U.S. Department of Education.

Nelson, C. (2003). Neural development and lifelong plasticity. In R. Lerner, F. Jacobs, & D. Wertlieb (Eds.), *Handbook of applied developmental science* (Vol. 1). Thousand Oaks, CA: Sage.

Oldenettel, D., & Wordes, M. (2000). *The community assessment center concept*. Washington, DC: U.S. Department of Justice, Office of Juvenile Justice and Delinquency Prevention.

Patterson, G. R. (1982). *Coercive family process.* Eugene, OR: Castalia.

Patterson, G. R., DeBaryshe, B. D., & Ramsey, E. (1989). A developmental perspective on antisocial behavior. *American Psychologist, 44,* 329–335.

Patterson, G. R., Reid, J. B., & Dishion, T. J. (1992). *Antisocial boys.* Eugene, OR: Castalia.

Pepler, D. J., & Craig, W. (2005). Aggressive girls on troubled trajectories: A developmental perspective. In D. J. Pepler, K. C. Madsen, C. Webster, & K. S. Levene (Eds.), *The development and treatment of girlhood aggression* (pp. 3–28). Mahwah, NJ: Erlbaum.

Pratt, J. (1989). Corporatism: The third model of juvenile justice. *British Journal of Criminology, 29,* 236–253.

Quay, H. C. (1966). Personality patterns in preadolescent delinquent boys. *Educational and Psychological Measurement, 16,* 99–110.

Quay, H. C. (1987). Patterns of delinquent behavior. In H. C. Quay (Ed.), *Handbook of juvenile delinquency* (pp. 118–138). New York: John Wiley.

Quinsey, V. L., Harris, G. T., Rice, M. E., & Cormier, C. A. (1998). *Violent offenders: Appraising and managing risk.* Washington, DC: American Psychological Association.

Redding, R. E., & Arrigo, B. (2005). Multicultural perspectives on delinquency among African-American youths: Etiology and intervention. In C. L. Frisby & C. R. Reynolds (Eds.), *A comprehensive handbook of multicultural school psychology* (pp. 710–743). New York: Wiley.

Reisig , M. D., Holtfreter, K., & Morash, M. (2006). Assessing recidivism risk across female pathways to crime. *Justice Quarterly, 23,* 384–405.

Rhee, S. H., & Waldman, I. D. (2002). Genetic and environmental influences on antisocial behavior: A meta-analysis of twin and adoption studies. *Psychological Bulletin, 128,* 490–529.

Rice, M., & Harris, G. T. (1995). Violent recidivism: Assessing predictive validity. *Journal of Consulting and Clinical Psychology, 63,* 737–748.

Rowe, D., Vazsonyi, A., & Flannery, D. (1995). Sex differences in crime: Do means and within-sex variation have similar causes? *Journal of Research in Crime and Delinquency, 32,* 84–101.

Rutter, M. (2000). Resilience reconsidered: Conceptual considerations, empirical findings, and policy implications. In J. P. Shonkoff & S. J. Meisels (Eds.), *Handbook of early childhood intervention* (pp. 651–682).Cambridge, UK: Cambridge University Press.

Rutter, M. (2003). Crucial paths from risk indicator to causal mechanism. In B. B. Lahey, T. E. Moffitt, & A. Caspi (Eds.), *Causes of conduct disorder and juvenile delinquency* (pp. 3–24). New York: Guilford.

Rutter, M., Giller, H., & Hagell, A. (1998). *Antisocial behavior by young people.* Cambridge, UK: Cambridge University Press.

Ryan, G., & Lane, S. (1997). *Juvenile sexual offending: Causes, consequences, and correction* (2nd ed.). California: Jossy-Bass.

Sampson, R. J., & Laub, J. H. (2005). A life-course view of the development of crime. *Annals of the American Academy of Political and Social Science, 602*, 12–45.

Sattler, J. M. (1998). *Clinical and forensic interviewing of children and families: Guidelines for the mental health, education, pediatric, and child maltreatment fields.* San Diego, CA: Sattler Publishing Company.

Sattler, J. M., & Hoge, R. D. (2006). *Assessment of children: Behavioral, social, and clinical foundations* (5th ed.). San Diego, CA: Sattler Publishing Company.

Schwalbe, C. S. (2007). Risk assessment for juvenile justice: A meta-analysis. *Law and Human Behavior, 31*, 449–462.

Schwalbe, C. S. (2008). A meta-analysis of juvenile justice risk assessment instruments: Predictive validity by gender. *Criminal Justice and Behavior, 35*, 1367–1381.

Schwartz, I. M. (Ed.). (1992). *Juvenile justice and public policy.* Lexington, MA: Lexington Books.

Scott, E., Reppucci, N., & Woolard, J. (1995). Evaluating adolescent decision making in legal contexts. *Law and Human Behavior, 19*, 221–244.

Scotti, J. R., Morris, T. L., McNeil, C. B., & Hawkins, R. P. (1996). DSM-IV and disorders of childhood and adolescence: Can structural criteria be functional? *Journal of Consulting and Clinical Psychology, 64*, 1177–1191.

Seagrave, D., & Grisso, T. (2002). Adolescent development and the measurement of juvenile psychopathy. *Law and Human Behavior, 26*, 219–239.

Shoemaker, D. J. (1996). *Theories of delinquency* (3rd ed.). New York: Oxford University Press.

Simourd, L., & Andrews, D. A. (1994). Correlates of delinquency: A look at gender differences. *Forum on Corrections Research, 6*, 26–31.

Snyder, H. N., & Sickmund, M. (1999). *Juvenile offenders and victims: 1999 national report.* Washington, DC: Office of Juvenile Justice Delinquency and Prevention, U.S. Department of Justice.

Surette, R. (1992). *Media, crime, and criminal justice: Images and realities.* Pacific Grove, CA: Brooks/Cole.

Tate, D. C., Reppucci, N. D., & Mulvey, E. P. (1995). Violent juvenile delinquents: Treatment effectiveness and implications for future action. *American Psychologist, 50*, 777–781.

Thornberry, T. P. (2005). Explaining multiple patterns of offending across the life course and across generations. *Annals of the American Academy of Political and Social Science, 602*, 156–195.

Tolan, P. H. (2007). Understanding violence. In D. J. Flannery, A. T. Vazsonyi, & I. D. Walman (Eds.), *The Cambridge handbook of violent behaviour and aggression* (pp. 5–18). Cambridge, UK: Cambridge University Press.

Tolan, P. H., & Gorman-Smith, D. (1998). Development of serious and violent offending careers. In R. Loeber & D. P. Farrington (Eds.), *Serious and violent juvenile offenders: Risk factors and successful interventions* (pp. 68–85). Thousand Oaks, CA: Sage.

Tolan, P. H., & Gorman-Smith, D. (2002). What violence prevention research can tell us about developmental psychopathology. *Development and Psychopathology, 14,* 713–729.

Tolan, P. H., & Guerra, N. G. (1994). *What works in reducing adolescent violence: An empirical review of the field.* Boulder, CO: Center for the Study and Prevention of Violence, University of Colorado.

Tolan, P. H., Guerra, N. G., & Kendall, P. H. (1995). A developmental-ecological perspective on antisocial behavior in children and adolescents: Toward a unified risk and intervention framework. *Journal of Consulting and Clinical Psychology, 63,* 577–584.

Turner, S. M., DeMers, S. T., Fox, H. R., & Reed, G. M. (2001). APA's guidelines for test user qualifications. *American Psychologist, 56,* 1099–1113.

Vincent, G., & Grisso, T. (2005). A developmental perspective on adolescent personality, psychopathology, and delinquency. In T. Grisso, G. Vincent, & D. Seagrave (Eds.), *Mental health screening and assessment in juvenile justice* (pp. 22–43). New York: Guilford.

Vitaro, F., & Brendgen, M. (2005). Proactive and reactive aggression: A developmental perspective. In R. E. Tremblay, W. W. Hartup, & J. Archer (Eds.), *Developmental origins of aggression* (pp. 178–201). New York: Guilford.

Warr, M. (2007). Violence and culture in the United States. In D. J. Flannery, A. T. Vazsonyi, & I. D. Waldman (Eds.), *The Cambridge handbook of violent behavior and aggression* (pp. 571–582). New York: Cambridge University Press.

Webster, C. D., Hucker, S., & Bloom, H. (2002). Transcending the actuarial versus clinical polemic in assessing risk for violence. *Criminal Justice and Behavior, 29,* 659–665.

West, D. J., & Farrington, D. P. (1977). *The delinquent way of life.* London: Heinemann.

Widom, C. S. (1994). Does violence beget violence? A critical examination of the literature. *Psychological Bulletin, 115,* 287–305.

Wiebush, R. G., Baird, C., Krisberg, B., & Onek, D. (1995). Risk assessment and classification for serious violent and chronic juvenile offenders. In J. C. Howell, B. Krisberg, J. D. Hawkins, & J. J. Wilson (Eds.),

A sourcebook: Serious, violent, and chronic juvenile offenders (pp. 171–212). Thousand Oaks, CA: Sage.

Williams, J. H., Ayers, C. D., Outlaw, W. S., Abbott, R. D., & Hawkins, J. D. (2001). The effects of race in juvenile justice: Investigating early stage processes. *Journal for Justice and Detention Services, 16,* 77–91.

Williams, K. R., Tuthill, L., & Lio, S. (2008). A portrait of juvenile offending in the United States. In R. D. Hoge, N. G. Guerra, & P. Boxer (Eds.), *Treating the juvenile offender* (pp. 15–32). New York: Guilford.

Wilson, J. J., & Howell, J. C. (1995). Comprehensive strategy for serious, violent, and chronic juvenile offenders. In J. C. Howell, B. Krisberg, J. D. Hawkins, & J. J. Wilson (Eds.), *A sourcebook: Serious, violent, and chronic juvenile offenders* (pp. 36–47). Thousand Oaks, CA: Sage.

World Health Organization. (1992). *The ICD-10 classification of mental and behavioural disorders: Clinical descriptions and diagnostic guidelines.* Geneva, Switzerland: Author.

Worling, J. R., & Langstrom, N. (2006). Risk of sexual recidivism in adolescents who offend sexually: Correlates and assessment. In H. E. Barbaree & W. L. Marshall (Eds.), *The juvenile sex offender* (2nd Edition) (pp. 219–247). New York: Guilford.

Zimring, F. E. (1998). *American youth violence.* New York: Oxford.

Tests and Specialized Tools

Attitudes Toward Institutional Authority (Gordon, 1993)

ADI: Adolescent Diagnostic Interview (Winters & Henley, 1993)

AJRAF: Arizona Juvenile Risk Assessment Form (Ashford, LeCroy, & Bond-Maupin, 1986)

APS: Adolescent Psychopathology Scale (Reynolds, 1998)

APSD: Antisocial Process Screening Device (Frick & Hare, 2001)

CAFAS: Child and Adolescent Functional Assessment Scale (Hodges, 2000)

CBCL: Child Behavior Checklist (CBCL; Achenbach & Rescorla, 2001)

CRS-R: Conners' Rating Scales—Revised (Conners, 1997)

CSS-M:Criminal Sentiments Scale—Modified (Simourd, 1997)

CTS: Criminal Thinking Scales (Knight, Garner, Simpson, Morey, Flynn, 2006)

DICA: Diagnostic Interview for Children and Adolescents (Reich, 2000)

DISC: Diagnostic Interview Schedule for Children (Shaffer, 1996)

DSMD: Devereux Scales of Mental Disorder (Naglieri, LeBuffe, & Pfeiffer, 1994)

EARL-20B: Early Assessment Risk Lists for Boys (Augimeri, Koegl, Webster, & Levene, 2001)

EARL-21G: Early Assessment Risk Lists for Girls (Levene et al., 2001)

ERASOR: Estimate of Risk of Adolescent Sexual Offense Recidivism (Worling & Curwen, 2000)

HIQ: Hostile Interpretations Questionnaire (Simourd & Mamuza, 2002)

HIT: How I Think Questionnaire (Gibbs, Barriga, & Potter, 2001)

Juvenile Probation and Aftercare Assessment Form (Baird, 1984, 1985)

JI-R: Jesness Inventory—Revised (Jesness, 1988, 2003)

LS/CMI:Level of Service/Case Management Inventory (Andrews, Bonta, & Wormith, 2004)

MacCAT-CA:MacArthur Competence Assessment Tool—Criminal Adjudication (Poythress et al., 1999)

MACI:Millon Adolescent Clinical Inventory (Millon, 1993)

MAYSI-2:The Massachusetts Youth Screening Instrument—Version 2 (Grisso & Barnum, 2003)

MMPI-A:Minnesota Multiphasic Personality Inventory—Adolescent (Butcher et al., 1992)

PCL-YV:Psychopathy Checklist—Youth Version (Forth, Kosson, & Hare, 2003)

PID:Pride in Delinquency Scale (Shields & Whitehall, 1991)

PIY:Personality Inventory for Youth (Lachar & Gruber, 1995)

POSIT:Problem-Oriented Screening Instrument for Teenagers (Rahdert, 1991)

RLAQ:Revised Legal Attitudes Questionnaire (Kravitz, Cutler, & Brock, 1993)

RBPC:Revised Behavior Problem Checklist (Quay & Peterson, 1996)

SAVRY:Structured Assessment of Violence Risk in Youth (Borum, Bartel, & Forth, 2006)

Washington State Juvenile Court Assessment (Barnoski, 2004)

WISC-IV:Wechsler Intelligence Scale for Children—Fourth Edition (Wechsler, 2004)

Youth Level of Service/Case Management Inventory (Hoge & Andrews, 2002; Hoge, 2005)

References for Tests and Specialized Tools

Achenbach, T. M., & Rescorla, L. A. (2001). *Manual for the ASEBA School-Age Forms and Profiles*. Burlington, VT: University of Vermont, Research Center for Children, Youth, and Families.

Andrews, D. A., Bonta, J., & Wormith, S. (2004). *Manual for the Level of Service/Case Management Inventory (LS/CMI)*. North Tonawanda, NY: Multi-Health Systems.

Ashford, J. B., LeCroy, C. W., & Bond-Maupin, L. (1986). *The Arizona juvenile aftercare decision making system*. Tempe, AZ: Arizona State University.

Augimeri, L. K., Koegl, C. J., Webster, C. D., & Levene, K. S. (2001). *Early assessment risk list for boys: EARL-20B. Version 2*. Toronto, ON: Earlscourt Child and Family Centre.

Baird, S. C. (1984). *Classification of juveniles in corrections: A model systems approach*. Washington, DC: Arthur D. Little.

Baird, S. C. (1985). Classifying juveniles: Making the most of an important management tool. *Corrections Today, 47*, 32–38.

Barnoski, R. (2004). *Assessing risk for re-offense: Validating the Washington State Juvenile Court Assessment* (Report No. 04-03-1201). Olympia, WA: Washington State Institute for Public Policy.

Borum, R., Bartel, P. A., & Forth, A. E. (2006). *Manual for the Structured Assessment of Violence Risk in Youth (SAVRY)*. Lutz, FL: PAR Associates.

Butcher, J. N., Williams, C. L., Graham, J. R., Archer, R. P., Tellegen, A., Ben-Porath, Y. S., et al. (1992). *Minnesota Multiphasic Personality Inventory—Adolescent*. Minneapolis, MN: University of Minnesota Press.

Conners, C. K. (1997). *The Conners Rating Scales—Revised: Technical manual*. North Tonawanda, NY: Multi-Health Systems.

Forth, A. E., Kosson, D. S., & Hare, R. D. (2003). *The Hare Psychopathy Checklist: Youth Version*. North Tonawanda, NY: Multi-Health Systems.

Frick, P. J., & Hare, R. (2001). *Antisocial Process Screening Device manual*. North Tonawanda, NY: Multi-Health Systems.

Gibbs, J. C., Barriga, A. Q., & Potter, G. B. (2001). *How I Think (HIT) questionnaire*. Champaign, IL: Research Press.

Gordon, L. V. (1993). *Manual for the Survey of Interpersonal Values*. Minneapolis, MN: National Computer Systems.

Grisso, T., & Barnum, R. (2003). *Massachusetts Youth Screening Instrument—Version 2: User's manual and technical report*. Sarasota, FL: Personal Resource Press.

Hodges, K. (2000). *Child and Adolescent Functional Assessment Scale*. Ypsilanti, MI: Eastern Michigan University.

Hoge, R. D. (2005). Youth Level of Service/Case Management Inventory. In T. Grisso, T. Vincent, & D. Seagrave (Eds.), *Mental health screening and assessment in juvenile justice* (pp. 283–294). New York: Guilford.

Hoge, R. D., & Andrews, D. A. (2002). *Youth Level of Service/Case Management Inventory user's manual*. North Tonawanda, NY: Multi-Health Systems.

Jesness, C. F. (1988). The Jesness Inventory classification system. *Criminal Justice and Behavior, 15*, 78–91.

Jesness, C. F. (2003). *Jesness Inventory—Revised.* North Tonawanda, NY: Multi-Health Systems.

Knight, K., Garner, B. R., Simpson, D. D., Morey, J. T., & Flynn, P. M. (2006). An assessment of criminal thinking. *Crime and Delinquency, 52,* 159–177.

Kravitz, D. A., Cutler, B. L., & Brock, P. (1993). Reliability and validity of the original and revised Legal Attitudes Questionnaire. *Law and Human Behavior, 17,* 661–667.

Lachar, D., & Gruber, C. P. (1995). *Personality Inventory for Youth.* Los Angeles, CA: Western Psychological Services.

Levene, K. S., Augimeri, L. K., Pepler, D., Walsh, M., Webster, C. D., & Koegl, C. J. (2001). *Early Assessment Risk List for Girls: EARL-21G, Version 1, Consultation Edition.* Toronto, ON: Earlscourt Child and Family Centre.

Millon, T. (1993). *Millon Adolescent Clinical Inventory.* Minneapolis, MN: National Computer Systems.

Naglieri, J. A., LeBuffe, P. A., & Pfeiffer, S. E. (1994). *Devereux Scales of Mental Disorders.* San Antonio, TX: The Psychological Corporation.

Poythress, N. G., Nicholson, R., Otto, R. K. Edens, J. F., Bonnie, R J., Monohan, J., et al. (1999). *Professional manual for the MacArthur Competence Assessment Tool—Criminal Adjudication.* Odessa, FL: Psychological Assessment Resources.

Quay, H. C., & Peterson, D. R. (1996). *Revised Behavior Problem Checklist professional manual.* Lutz, FL: Psychological Assessment Resources.

Rahdert, E. R. (1991). *The Adolescent assessment/referral system.* Rockville, MD: National Institute on Drug Abuse.

Reich, W. (2000). Diagnostic Interview Schedule for Children and Adolescents. *Journal of the American Academy of Child and Adolescent Psychiatry, 39,* 59–66.

Reynolds, W. M. (1998). *Adolescent Psychopathology Scale.* Lutz, FL: Psychological Assessment Resources.

Shaffer, D. (1996). *Diagnostic Interview Schedule for Children (DISC–4).* New York: New York State Psychiatric Institute.

Shields, I., & Whitehall, G. C. (1991). *The Pride in Delinquency Scale.* Ottawa, ON: Department of Psychology, Carleton University.

Simourd, D. J. (1997). The Criminal Sentiments Scale-Modified and Pride in Delinquency Scale: Psychometric properties and construct validity of two measures of criminal attitudes. *Criminal Justice and Behavior, 24,* 52–70.

Simourd, D. J., & Mamuza, J. M. (2002). *Hostile Interpretations Questionnaire User's manual.* Kingston, ON: ACES.

Wechsler, D. (2004). *Wechsler Intelligence Scale for Children* (4th ed.). San Antonio, TX: The Psychological Corporation.

Winters, K., & Henley, G. (1993). *Adolescent Diagnostic Interview manual.* Los Angeles, CA: Western Psychological Services.

Worling, J. R., & Curwen, M. A. (2001). *Estimate of Risk of Adolescent Sexual Offense Recidivism (ERASOR).* Toronto, ON: Thistletown Regional Centre.

Cases and Statutes

In re Gault, 387 US 1, 87 S Ct. 1428, 18 L. Ed. 2nd 527 (1967).

Kent v. United States, 383 US 541, 86 S.Ct 1045, 16 L.Ed.2d 84 (1966).

Key Terms

actuarial assessments: a formal method that uses an equation, formula, or actuarial table to arrive at a probability, or expected value, of some outcome.

adolescent-limited trajectory: describes a pattern where behavior develops normally until adolescence when antisocial actions first appear.

aggressive act: any intentional action causing harm to another.

callous and unemotional traits: characterize youth who seem incapable of experiencing empathy or of forming normal social attachments.

clinical judgments: judgments based solely on informal and subjective processes.

concurrent validity: form of criterion-related validity where assessment and criterion scores are collected at the same time.

conduct disorder: condition associated with frequent engagement in antisocial actions resulting in harm to self or others; examples include violence, lying, stealing.

construct validity: form of validity referring to the theoretical meaning or accuracy of a measure.

contingency tables: tables expressing the frequencies or percentages of true and false predictions.

criterion-referenced: scores expressed relative to a standard of performance; for example, a score expressed as percentage of items correct.

criterion-related validity: form of validity referring to links between scores and behavioral or performance criteria.

distal factors: risk factors that operate more remotely and have an impact through the proximal factors. Examples include financial problems in the family and negative neighborhood environment.

dynamic risk factors: variables subject to change over time or through planned interventions that affect an individual's likelihood of some target behavior such as violence or sexual violence. (Also see *needs assessment*.)

false negatives: predict negative outcome but obtain positive.

false positives: predict positive outcome but obtain negative.

internal consistency: method for evaluating reliability based on an analysis of relations among items within the measure.

inter-rater agreement: method for evaluating reliability based on comparing scores from multiple raters.

just deserts: term referring to the assumption that punishment should fit the crime.

life-course-persistent: describes a pattern whereby conduct disorders appear during childhood, followed by persistent criminal activity through adolescence and adult years.

needs assessment: identifying variables subject to change over time or through planned intervention that affect an individual's likelihood of some target behavior such as violence or sexual violence; also referred to as dynamic risk factors.

normative-referenced: scores expressed relative to the performance of a normative sample; for example, a score indicating that the individual scored one deviation above the mean of the sample.

normative scores: scores expressed relative to a normative sample of individuals.

oppositional-defiant disorder: condition associated with persistent refusal to follow instructions or rules.

parens patriae: a legal philosophy that affords courts the discretion of a benevolent parent and allows decisions to be based on the "best interests of the child."

prediction: a prediction of the likelihood that the individual will engage in a target behavior in the future, such as a criminal act.

predictive validity: form of criterion-related validity where assessment scores are collected at one time and criterion scores are collected at a future time.

prevalence: the number of youth within a particular sample engaging in criminal activity.

proactive: aggressive acts that are goal directed and motivated by a perception that the action will lead to a desirable reward.

proximal factors: risk factors that have a direct effect on criminal activity (e.g., inadequate parenting, substance abuse, antisocial attitudes).

psychopathy: a specific form of personality disorder, not included in the DSM-IV-TR, involving a callous, egocentric personality style, coupled with an impulsive, chronically antisocial lifestyle.

rates: the incidence or prevalence of criminal activity within a particular sample or region.

reactive: aggressive act motivated by anger in response to real or perceived threats.

reliability: the extent to which error variance contributes to a score.

responsivity: variables relating to the individual or his circumstances not directly related to the criminal activity but that should be taken into account in case planning.

risk assessment: identifying factors affecting the likelihood of engaging in antisocial acts and the probability that such acts will occur.

risk management: developing and implementing strategies for addressing criminogenic needs and thereby reducing the risk of reoffending.

screening instruments: assessment tools designed to provide initial information about risk and need factors; generally simple to administer and interpret.

standardized assessment: assessment tools with established content and scoring procedures.

static risk factors: variables that are historical or do not change through planned intervention and that are related to an individual's likelihood of some future activity, such as violence or sexual violence.

strength: resilience or protective factors that moderate the effects of risk factors.

structured professional judgments: clinical judgments anchored by standardized assessment tools.

test–retest: method for evaluating reliability based on comparing scores from two or more administrations of a measure.

true negatives: negative prediction and negative outcome.

true positives: positive prediction and positive outcome.

validity: generally refers to the meaningfulness of a measure; encompasses a number of different forms of validity.

violent act: aggressive act causing physical harm to another.

Index

About the Authors

Robert D. Hoge, PhD, is Professor Emeritus of Psychology and Distinguished Research Professor at Carleton University in Ottawa where he is involved in teaching and research in child and adolescent psychology, forensic psychology, and psychological assessment. He has served as a consultant to numerous government and private agencies, including the National Parole Board of Canada, Justice Canada, Ontario Ministry of Community and Social Services, Alaska Division of Juvenile Justice, Florida Department of Juvenile Justice, the United Nations Institute of Crime and Crime Prevention, and the Governments of Singapore and Bermuda. Dr. Hoge has published extensively in Canadian and international journals. His books include *Assessing the Youthful Offender: Issues and Techniques* (with D. A. Andrews, 1996), *Assessing Adolescents in Educational, Counseling, and Other Settings* (1999), *The Juvenile Offender: Theory, Research, and Applications* (2001), *Assessment of Children: Behavioral, Social, and Clinical Foundations—Fifth Edition* (with J. Sattler, 2005), and *Treatment of the Juvenile Offender* (with N. Guerra & P. Boxer, 2008). He is also coauthor with Dr. Andrews of the *Youth Level of Service/Case Management Inventory* (Multi-Health Systems), a widely used risk/need assessment tool. Dr. Hoge is a Fellow of the Canadian Psychological Association and a registered psychologist in the Province of Ontario, with a specialty in forensic psychology.

D. A. Andrews, PhD, is Professor Emeritus and Distinguished Research Professor in the Department of Psychology and in the Institute of Criminology and Criminal Justice at Carleton University, Ottawa, Ontario. He is interested in the assessment and treatment of criminal offenders, the psychology of criminal conduct, and the social psychology of textbook criminological knowledge. His primary theoretical orientation is a general personality and cognitive social learning perspective. Dr. Andrews has published numerous widely cited journal articles. His books include *The Psychology of Criminal Conduct* (with James Bonta) and *Assessing the Juvenile Offender: Issues and Techniques* (with Robert D. Hoge). He is also co-author with James Bonta and Steve Wormith of the *Level of Service/Case Management Inventory*, a widely used risk/need assessment instrument. Dr. Andrews has served as a consultant to a wide range of judicial and correctional systems and has been the recipient of numerous professional honors.